DORLING KINDERSLEY DK EYEWITNESS BOOKS

HORSE

Kulan

Woman and girl
wearing Spanish
riding costumes,
on dapple gray
Andalusian

Bronze
statuette of
warrior on
horseback,
c. 550 B.C.

Brass rowel spur, from
South America, c. 1800

Henry VIII's full-horse armor

Mule drawing
Indian cart, c. 1840

Bronze plaque
of warrior on
horseback, from
Benin, Nigeria,
late 16th century

Foot and two side toes of *Anchitherium* fossil

HORSE

Old shoe and nails removed from horse's hoof

Written by
JULIET CLUTTON-BROCK

Mountain zebra

Shoeing a Shire horse

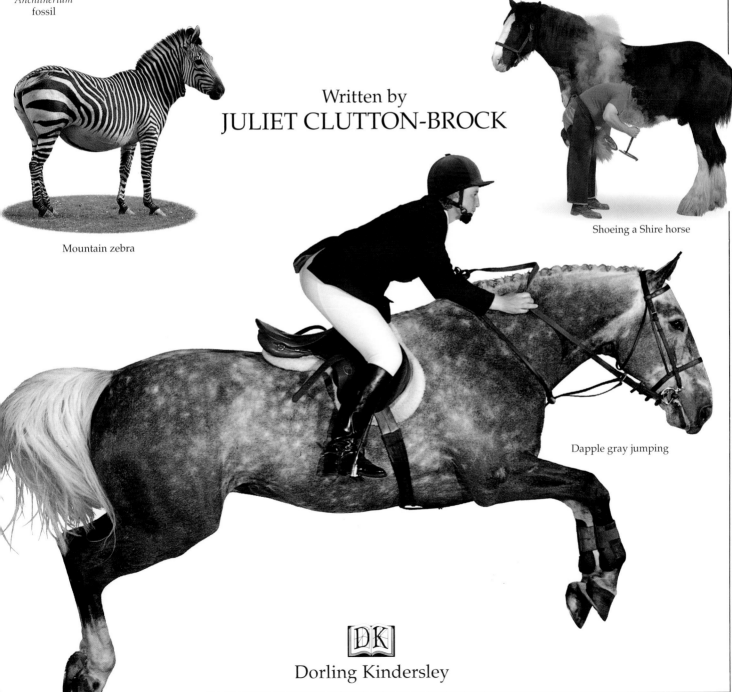

Dapple gray jumping

Dorling Kindersley

Drum horse
and rider

Irish donkey
pulling cart, c. 1850

DK
Dorling Kindersley
**LONDON, NEW YORK, AUCKLAND, DELHI,
JOHANNESBURG, MUNICH, PARIS and SYDNEY**

For a full catalog, visit
DK www.dk.com

Project editor Marion Dent
Art editor Jutta Kaiser-Atcherley
Senior editor Helen Parker
Senior art editor Julia Harris
Production Louise Barratt
Picture research Diana Morris
Special photography Jerry Young and Karl Shone

This Eyewitness ® Book has been conceived by
Dorling Kindersley Limited and Editions Gallimard

© 1992 Dorling Kindersley Limited
This edition © 2000 Dorling Kindersley Limited
First American edition, 1992

Published in the United States by
Dorling Kindersley Publishing, Inc.
375 Hudson Street,
New York, NY 10014
8 10 9 7

Two wild Przewalski horses

Archer on horseback,
c. 5th century B.C.

Dorling Kindersley books are available at special discounts for bulk
purchases for sales promotions or premiums. Special editions, including
personalized covers, excerpts of existing guides, and corporate imprints
can be created in large quantities for specific needs. For more information,
contact Special Markets Dept., Dorling Kindersley Publishing, Inc.

French-style barouche, c. 1880

Library of Congress Cataloging-in-Publication Data
Clutton-Brock, Juliet.
Horse / written by Juliet Clutton-Brock.
p. cm. — (Eyewitness Books)
Includes index.
Summary: A photo essay introducing members of the horse
family, their evolution, behavior, importance, history,
breeding, and training. Includes major international
breeds of domestic horses.
1. Horses — Juvenile literature.
2. Equus — Juvenile literature.
3. Horse breeds — Juvenile literature.
[1. Equidae. 2. Horses. 3. Horse breeds.]
I. Young, Jerry, ill. II. Title.
SF302C6 2000   636.1—dc20 91-53132
ISBN 0-7894-5773-3 (pb)
ISBN 0-7894-5772-5 (hc)

Palomino with
Western-style
bridle and saddle

Color reproduction by Colourscan, Singapore
Printed in China by Toppan Printing Co. (Shenzhen) Ltd.

Pair of
grays with
phaeton, c. 1840

Contents

Pair of Gelderlands
pulling covered wagon

6
The horse family
8
How horses evolved
10
Bones and teeth
12
Senses and behavior
14
Mares and foals
16
Wild asses
18
Seeing stripes
20
Ancient ancestors
22
Horses in history
24
Donkey work
26
Mules and hinnies
28
Shoes and shoeing
30
Bits and pieces
32
Exploring by horse
34
To the Americas
36
Running wild
38
Horses from around the world

40
More breeds and colors
42
War-horses
44
The age of chivalry
46
Traveling by horse
48
Horse-drawn vehicles
50
Heavy horses
52
Horse power
54
Light draft work
56
The horse in North America
58
Sporting horses
60
Horses for courses
62
Useful ponies
64
Index

The horse family

Horses, asses, and zebras all belong to one family of mammals called the Equidae. They are called "odd-toed" animals because they have only one hoof on each foot; cows and deer have two hooves and are called "even-toed." The Equidae are classified in the order Perissodactyla with their nearest relatives, the rhinoceroses and tapirs. All members of the horse family (equids) feed by grazing on grasses and shrubs. They live in open country and are fast-running animals that depend on speed to escape predators. All are highly social (pp. 12–13) and live in family groups that join together into a herd. They travel over great distances in search of food or water or to get away from flies and mosquitoes, which plague them in hot weather. Although there is great variation in size between different breeds of domestic horse (pp. 38–41), they all belong to one species – *Equus caballus*. A pony is defined as a horse that has a height of less than 14.2 hands (58 in/147 cm). Various parts of a horse all have different names and are called the "points" of the horse.

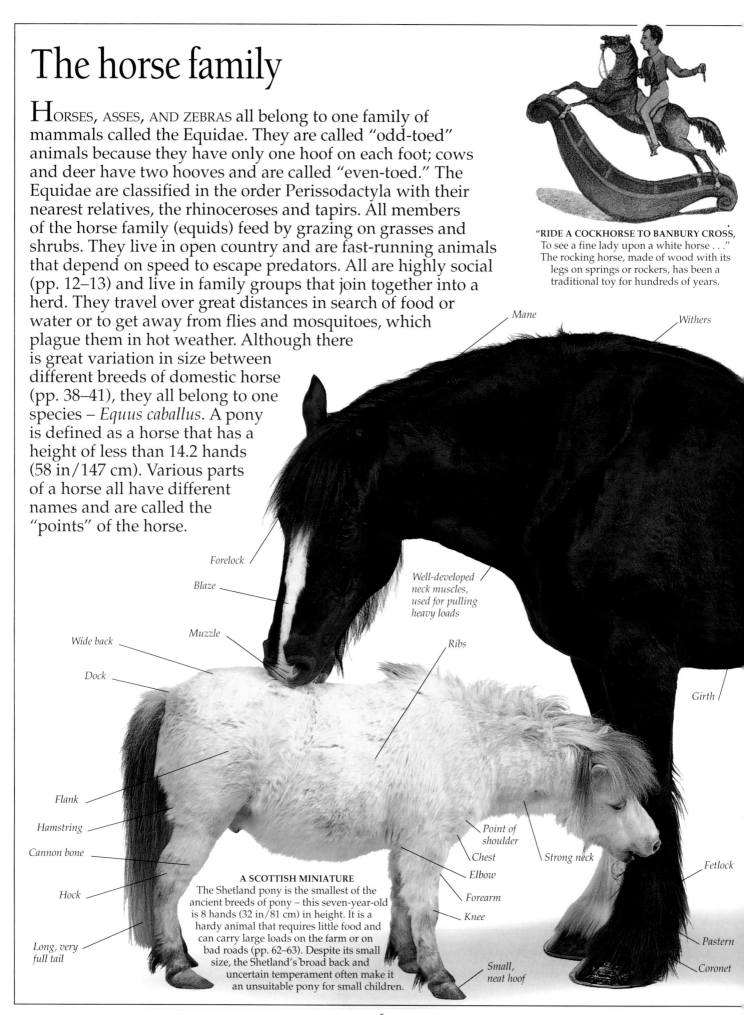

"RIDE A COCKHORSE TO BANBURY CROSS,
To see a fine lady upon a white horse . . ."
The rocking horse, made of wood with its legs on springs or rockers, has been a traditional toy for hundreds of years.

Mane

Withers

Forelock

Blaze

Muzzle

Well-developed neck muscles, used for pulling heavy loads

Ribs

Wide back

Dock

Girth

Flank

Hamstring

Cannon bone

Hock

Point of shoulder

Chest

Elbow

Forearm

Knee

Strong neck

Fetlock

Pastern

Coronet

Small, neat hoof

Long, very full tail

A SCOTTISH MINIATURE
The Shetland pony is the smallest of the ancient breeds of pony – this seven-year-old is 8 hands (32 in/81 cm) in height. It is a hardy animal that requires little food and can carry large loads on the farm or on bad roads (pp. 62–63). Despite its small size, the Shetland's broad back and uncertain temperament often make it an unsuitable pony for small children.

Large ears with
dark tips

No forelock

Short, erect mane

Long,
erect ears

Typical white
muzzle

Pale brown shadow
striping between
black stripes

Heavy head

Dark muzzle

Dark
muzzle

ASSES AND ZEBRAS
Besides the horse, the other members of
the horse family are the Asian wild asses,
or onagers (pp. 16–17); the African wild
ass (pp. 16–17), which is the ancestor of
the domestic donkey (pp. 24–25); and the
zebras (pp. 18–19).

Pale
underbelly

Kulan – a type of
Asian wild ass

Poitou
donkey

Common or
plains zebra
mother and foal

Broad back

Very powerful
rump

How to measure a horse's height
The height of a horse is measured in hands. One hand, literally
the width of an adult's hand, is equal to 4 in (10.16 cm). If a
horse measures 15.2 hands, then it is 62 in (157 cm) high. This
measurement is taken from its feet to the top of its shoulders,
which are called the withers.

Tail is often
docked

A GREAT HORSE
The Shire horse was first bred in
the English Midlands for work
on farms and for pulling heavy
loads (pp. 50–53). This breed is
distinguished by its huge size
and by the long hair, or
"feathering," around the feet.
The horse shown here is
named King, and he holds
the record for the tallest
horse in the world. His
height at the withers is
19.2 hands (78 in/198 cm).

Feathered feet

HORNED HEAD
A unicorn is a mythical horse that
had a long horn growing out of its forehead.
On armor in Medieval times, this "horse" had a
lion's tail, two-toed hooves, and a spiraled horn.

Huge hoof

EUROPEAN TRAVELERS
Africa has given the world many members of the
horse family – from zebras to wild asses. As
Europeans explored this vast continent, they
brought their domesticated horses with them to
use as transportation. This elaborate wood carving
of human and animal figures (including horses)
was made by Ibo people in Nigeria, West Africa.

How horses evolved

Iᴛ ᴛᴏᴏᴋ ᴀʙᴏᴜᴛ 55 ᴍɪʟʟɪᴏɴ ʏᴇᴀʀs for the present family of horses, asses, and zebras (equids) to evolve (gradually change) from their earliest horselike ancestor. Originally called *Eohippus*, or "dawn horse" – because it lived during the Eocene epoch – it is now known as *Hyracotherium*. This early horse was not much larger than a hare. It was a "browsing" animal – which fed on leaves and shrubs – and had four hoofed toes on its front feet and three on its hind feet. It lived in the woodlands of Europe, North America, and eastern Asia. Gradually, over millions of years, this small animal evolved into a "grazing" (grass-eating) mammal with three hoofed toes, and later, with a single hoof, on all feet. At first, browsing horses, like *Mesohippus* and then *Parahippus*, had low-crowned teeth (pp. 10–11), but during the later Miocene epoch (20 million years ago) grasslands began to replace the woodlands in North America. In adapting to this new environment, ancestral horses evolved longer limbs that enabled them to range over a wide area in search of pasture and to escape from predators. At the same time, their teeth became high-crowned in order to adapt to their diet of tough grasses. The first grazing horse was *Merychippus*, but eventually it was replaced by *Pliohippus*, the first one-toed horse. This gave rise to *Equus* during the Pleistocene (about two million years ago).

Side toe

Hoof of side toe

Main hoof core

Side view of left hind foot of *Hipparion*

Left side toe

Right side toe

Hoof of small side toe

Main hoof core

Front view of hind foot of *Hipparion*

Nasal bone

SOUTH AMERICAN HORSE
This is the skeleton of *Hippidion*, an extinct one-toed equid that evolved in Central America and then spread into South America. Its descendant, *Onohippidium*, survived in South America until at least 12,000 years ago, when their extinction may have been hastened by the first human hunters traveling through the continent at the end of the ice age.

Ear bone

Orbit, or eye socket

LAST OF THE THREE-TOED HORSES
Hipparion (side view of skull, above) was the last of the three-toed equids. It was a very successful grazer with high-crowned teeth, and its fossil remains have been found in many parts of Europe, Asia, and Africa. *Hipparion* did not finally become extinct in Africa until about 125,000 years ago.

Incisor for cutting food

Lost incisor

Four-toed

Three-toed

Three-toed

Three-toed

One-toed

Hyracotherium

Mesohippus

Parahippus

Merychippus

Pliohippus

BROWSERS

GRAZERS

EQUINE SIDELINE
The three-toed fossil horse *Anchitherium* was very successful and spread from America through Asia and Europe in the early Miocene epoch (about 24 million years ago). However, it was an equine sideline – that is, one that did not evolve into the modern horse. It became extinct before the beginning of the Pliocene epoch, about five million years ago.

Side toe

Side toe – hoof core missing

Side hoof core

Main hoof core

Foot and toe bones of *Anchitherium*

Lower cheek teeth (molars and premolars)

Lower jaw of *Anchitherium*

Part of mandible (jaw bone)

Upper cheek teeth

Upper jaw of *Anchitherium*

Orbit, or eye socket

Palatal bone

Cranium for brain

Ear bone

Base of skull

Palatal view of *Hyracotherium* skull, showing roof of mouth

THE OLDEST EQUID
The palatal (roof of mouth) view of the skull of a fossil *Hyracotherium* from the Eocene epoch (54 million years ago) in England shows the square, six-lobed teeth that were the foundation from which the teeth of modern horses evolved.

Ear bone

Orbit

Nasal bone

Cheek teeth

Side view of right half of *Hyracotherium* skull

High-crowned teeth used for grazing

Foramen magnum (hole for spinal cord)

Orbit

Cranium

Ear bone

Palatal view of *Hipparion* skull

One-toed

Equus

GRAZERS

FIRST THREE-TOED HORSE
Mesohippus, which lived during the Oligocene epoch about 37 million years ago, was the first horse to have three toes (with the middle toe larger than the two side ones) and was the same size as a sheep.

Cranium

Eye socket

Upper molar

Nose bone

Upper premolar

Incisor, used for cutting food

Lower premolar

Mandible, or lower jaw

Atlas, or first cervical vertebra

Axis, or second cervical vertebra

Teeth of 20-year-old horse showing signs of wear

Neck vertebra

Scapula, or shoulder blade

LONG IN THE TOOTH
As a horse grows older, the shape of its incisors change from oval to round to triangular and then to a flat four-sided shape. Also with age, a horse's gums recede (so that it becomes "long in the tooth"), and its teeth wear down. With all these indicators, experts can tell how old a horse is.

Humerus

Bones and teeth

Aɴ ᴇǫᴜɪᴅ's sᴋᴇʟᴇᴛᴏɴ is built for speed and stamina. All wild equids range over huge areas of open grassland; they gallop fast and have extraordinarily sharp eyesight, which helps them to escape predators. The skull of the horse is very long and contains a great battery of grinding teeth that are used for chewing grass. The vertebral column (backbone) keeps the back rigid, the rib cage protects the heart and lungs, and the leg bones are very long. A distinguishing feature of the equids is that they run on only a single toe. This is equivalent to the third finger, or toe, of a human; toes two and four are reduced to thin splint bones, and toes one and five are lost altogether. When a foal is born, it may be toothless, but the milk or baby teeth soon erupt through the soft jawbones. Milk teeth are temporary and, in time, are replaced by adult or permanent teeth. An adult male equid usually has 40 teeth – 12 incisors, 4 canines, 12 premolars, and 12 molars – but in the female the canines are very small. As horses age, their teeth gradually wear down, change shape, and become very discolored.

CLASSIC SKELETON
In 1766 English artist George Stubbs (1724–1806) published a book titled *The Anatomy of the Horse*, which is still used as a classic work of reference more than 200 years later. In order to show the horse's bone construction accurately, he had to dissect a great number of horses.

Radius

Knee

Metacarpal or front cannon bone

First phalanx or long pastern bone

Second phalanx or short pastern bone

Hoof

Skeleton of a racehorse

STRAIGHT FROM THE HORSE'S MOUTH
Like all mammals, the foal has a set of milk teeth. Milk teeth are worn down as the foal is weaned off milk and begins to graze; they are replaced by adult teeth. At first, the adult teeth have short roots and very long crowns, which gradually wear down throughout the life of the horse.

Adult molar starting to develop

Milk premolar

Milk canine

Milk incisor

Upper jaw of newborn horse

Adult molar starting to develop

Adult molar, ready for cutting

Milk premolar

Adult premolar

Milk incisor

Upper jaw of two-year-old pony

Upper jaw of six-year-old pony

Molar, for grinding food

Premolar, for chewing food

Incisor, for cutting food

Molar almost worn away

Premolar

Incisor

Upper jaw of very aged horse

Spinal vertebra

Hipbone

Pelvic girdle

Femur

Coccygeal or tail vertebra

Rib

Stifle joint

Fibula

Tibia

Hock joint

COMPLICATED MUSCLE STRUCTURE
This skillful anatomical drawing by George Stubbs shows the amazing muscle structure of the horse, which enables it to travel very long distances (pp. 46–49), to jump great heights (pp. 58–59), and to haul heavy loads (pp. 50–53).

Metatarsal or hind cannon bone

AN OLD CHESTNUT
There are around 25 species of the horse chestnut tree in North America, Europe, and Asia. In the late 1500s the seeds apparently were used for treating respiratory illnesses in horses, and this is how the tree got its name. The spiny capsules enclose large seeds, the scar of which resembles a horse's hoof and even seems to show the holes for the nails.

First phalanx

Second phalanx

Hoof

SPEED AND STAMINA
The shape of a horse's skeleton depends on its breed. A cart horse has massive bones that support its huge muscles, which are used for hauling great weights; a racehorse (shown here) has long, slender bones that are built for speed. But the bones must not be too light or they will break under the stress of the racetrack.

Senses and behavior

Ears pointing back show anger or fear

Ears pointing forward show interest in surroundings

HORSES, ASSES, AND ZEBRAS all have more highly developed senses of sight, hearing, and smell than humans. The characteristic long face of the horse holds not only the large teeth but also the sensitive organs of smell. The eyes are set far up in the skull and are positioned on the sides of the head, so the horse has good all-around vision, even when it is grazing. The ears are large – and in asses very long – and can be moved around and pointed toward the slightest sound. By nature the horse is a herd animal and shows great affection toward other members of its group, and this loyalty is easily transferred to its human owner. Once this bond is developed, the horse will try very hard to follow commands, however harsh. As a result, horses have been cruelly used but also deeply loved, possibly more than any other animal in human history. Despite their close association with humans, the domestic horse and donkey still retain the instincts and natural behavioral patterns of their wild ancestors. They will defend their territory and suckle their foals in just the same way as will the wild horse and the wild ass, and they will always need companionship.

ROLLING OVER
This pony is having a good roll, which is an important part of grooming. It relaxes the muscles and helps to remove loose hair, dirt, and parasites.

One ear forward, one ear back shows uncertainty

TWO-WAY STRETCH
An equid's ears have a dual role – to pick up sounds and to transmit visual signals. If a mule (shown here) lays its ears back, it is frightened or angry. If they are forward, then it is interested in what is happening around it, such as the clatter of a food bucket. One ear forward and one back means it is not sure what will happen next.

Ears laid back, showing anger

Kick

KICKING KULANS
The laid-back ears and threatening kicks show that these kulans, or onagers (pp. 16–17), are not getting along too well.

Zebra calling, to warn other animals in the herd of danger

PROTECTING TERRITORY AND FAMILY
Fighting by rearing and stabbing with their front hooves is natural to all equids. However, they may prefer to settle their differences by threats with their ears, tails, and feet and by using other body language. Stallions and geldings (sterilized males) will fight over territory or to protect their mares, as shown by these Icelandic ponies.

FLEHMEN REACTION
By pulling back his lips and
drawing air in over his vomero-
nasal, or Jacobson's, organ after
smelling a mare's urine, this stallion
is testing whether she is in heat (in
oestrus) – that is, whether she is ready to mate.
This is called the flehmen reaction.

Lead horse, ignoring his driver's commands,
takes the liberty of stopping for a drink

THE BEST OF FRIENDS
Two horses will often stand close together, head to
tail, nuzzling each other's manes and backs, thus
establishing their relationship. The frequency of
these grooming and cleaning sessions varies
from season to season, but they usually
last around three minutes.

*Ears laid back
showing shock
of bite
attack*

*Biting an
unfamiliar
horse*

A BITE THREAT
These Przewalski
horses (pp. 20–21), from
two different herds, are
trying to show who is
the more important,
or dominant. The
attacking horse's
neck is thrust
forward to bite
its opponent.

Mares and foals

A MARE, OR FEMALE HORSE, ASS, OR ZEBRA usually gives birth to one foal after a gestation period, or carrying time, of 11 months or a little longer. The mares mate with a stallion in spring; all the foals are then born the following spring when there is fresh grass. The gestation period is as long as a year because the mother must produce a healthy, well-developed foal (or very rarely twins); the foal can walk within an hour after birth and can soon keep up with the moving herd. Although the mare will continue to suckle her foal for up to a year, the foal begins to graze after a few weeks. Asses (pp. 16–17), zebras (pp. 18–19), and horses are all grazers that live on open grasslands where food can be scarce, and young animals could be an easy target for large predators, such as lions in Africa. Between the ages of one and four years, a female foal is called a filly and a male foal a colt. In the wild, fillies and colts leave their mothers' herds and form new groups of their own when they mature.

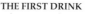

A PREGNANT PALOMINO
This Palomino (pp. 38–39) shows by her large belly that she will soon give birth. Both feral and domestic mares (pp. 36–37) tend to give birth quickly, but highly bred horses are usually carefully watched in case something goes wrong.

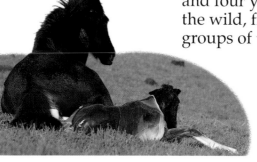

A NEWBORN FOAL
This mare is resting for a few minutes after giving birth to her foal, which still has part of the amniotic or birth sac over its back. Soon the foal will kick free from its mother, breaking off the umbilical cord, which has provided it with nourishment up to now in the uterus (womb).

LICKING INTO SHAPE
The mare gets to her feet and removes the birth sac by licking the foal all over. This also helps strengthen the foal's circulation and breathing.

Foal's erect ears showing alertness

MOTHER AND FOAL
It will take almost three years for the young foal of this common zebra (pp. 18–19) to become as large as its mother. The family bonds of zebras are very strong, and all the adults combine to protect their foals from danger.

Mother nudging foal away from danger

Six-year-old common zebra mother and three-month-old foal

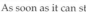

THE FIRST DRINK
As soon as it can stand, the foal will search for the mother's teats between her hind legs and will begin to suck. The first milk is called colostrum, and it helps the foal build up lifelong immunity to disease.

STANDING ON ITS OWN FOUR FEET
While the mother looks around for danger, the foal takes its first faltering steps.

WATCH OUT!
Although this Shire mare (pp. 50–53) is descended from horses that have been domesticated for thousands of years (pp. 22–23), she still has the instincts of her wild ancestors and will be constantly on guard against possible danger to her foal.

Alert ears listening for signs of danger

Mother's muzzle protecting foal

Height at withers 11.2 hands (46 in/117 cm)

KEEPING UP
A foal is on its feet within an hour of birth, and it must try to keep up with its mother – particularly in the wild.

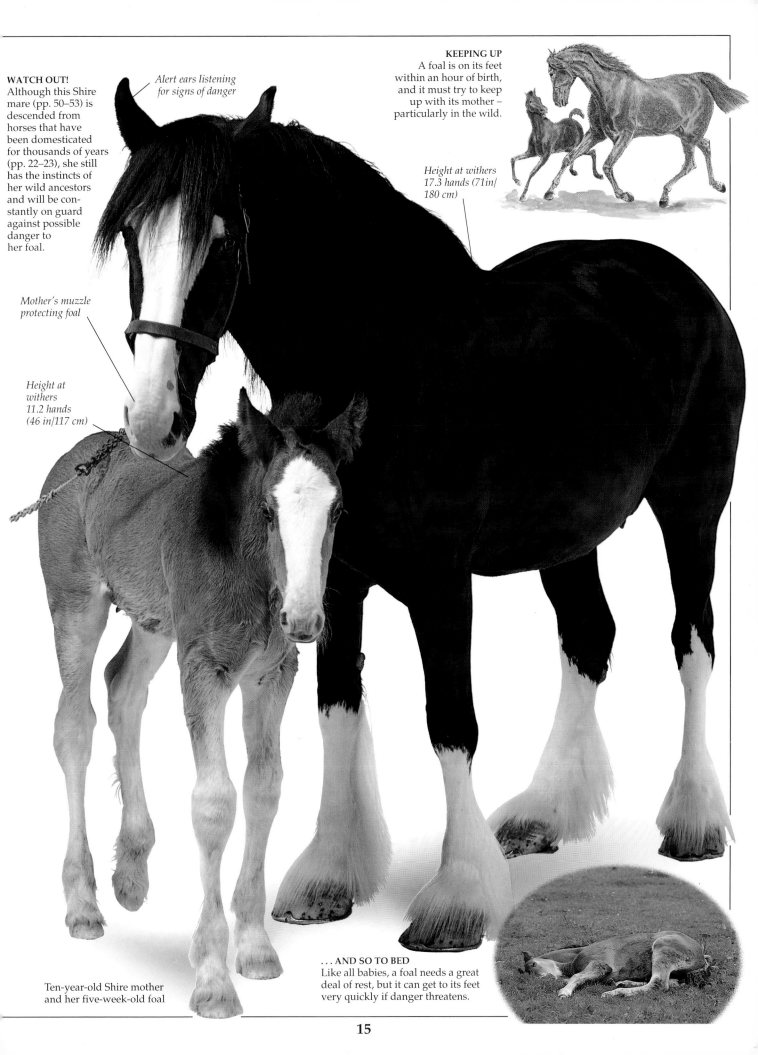

Height at withers 17.3 hands (71in/ 180 cm)

Ten-year-old Shire mother and her five-week-old foal

. . . AND SO TO BED
Like all babies, a foal needs a great deal of rest, but it can get to its feet very quickly if danger threatens.

Wild asses

THERE ARE THREE SPECIES of wild ass, and they are no more closely related to one another than the horse is to the zebra. They can interbreed, but their off-spring will be infertile (pp. 18–19). The three species are the true wild ass of Africa (*Equus africanus*), which until recently ranged over the Sahara Desert in North Africa, and the two species of Asian wild asses – the onager (*Equus hemionus*) from the Middle East and northwest India, and the kiang (*Equus kiang*) from the Tibetan plateau, north of the Himalayas. Of these three species, it is the African wild ass that is the ancestor of the domestic donkey (pp. 24–25). All wild asses look similar – a heavy head, long ears, a short mane, no forelock, slender legs, and a wispy tail. The African wild ass is grayish in color, with a white belly and a dark stripe along its back; it often has horizontal stripes around its legs and a black stripe over its shoulders. The Asian wild asses are redder in color and never have leg or shoulder stripes, though they do have a dark line along the back. All wild asses are adapted for life in the arid, rocky environment of the semideserts and mountain plateaus of Africa and Asia, where they graze on thornbushes and dry grass. Today, all wild asses are in danger of extinction from loss of their habitat and overhunting by humans.

FIRST CATCH YOUR ONAGER
The above scenes of catching wild onagers alive (c. 645 B.C.) are from the stone friezes that adorned the palace of Nineveh in Assyria. These Syrian onagers (now extinct) were perhaps being caught for crossbreeding (pp. 26–27) with domestic donkeys or horses.

Long, wispy tail

PRESERVATION
Until recently, there were several races of African wild asses. The Somali wild ass (*Equus africanus somalinensis*), the only African ass still to survive in the wild, usually has stripes around its legs, but not its shoulder. These asses have been taken to a wildlife reserve in Israel to try to save the species, whose home is in war-torn Ethiopia and Somalia.

Slender, pale-colored leg

NOW EXTINCT
The Nubian wild ass (*Equus africanus africanus*) is now extinct. It differed from the Somali ass in that it had a very short, dark stripe across its shoulders but no horizontal stripes on its legs.

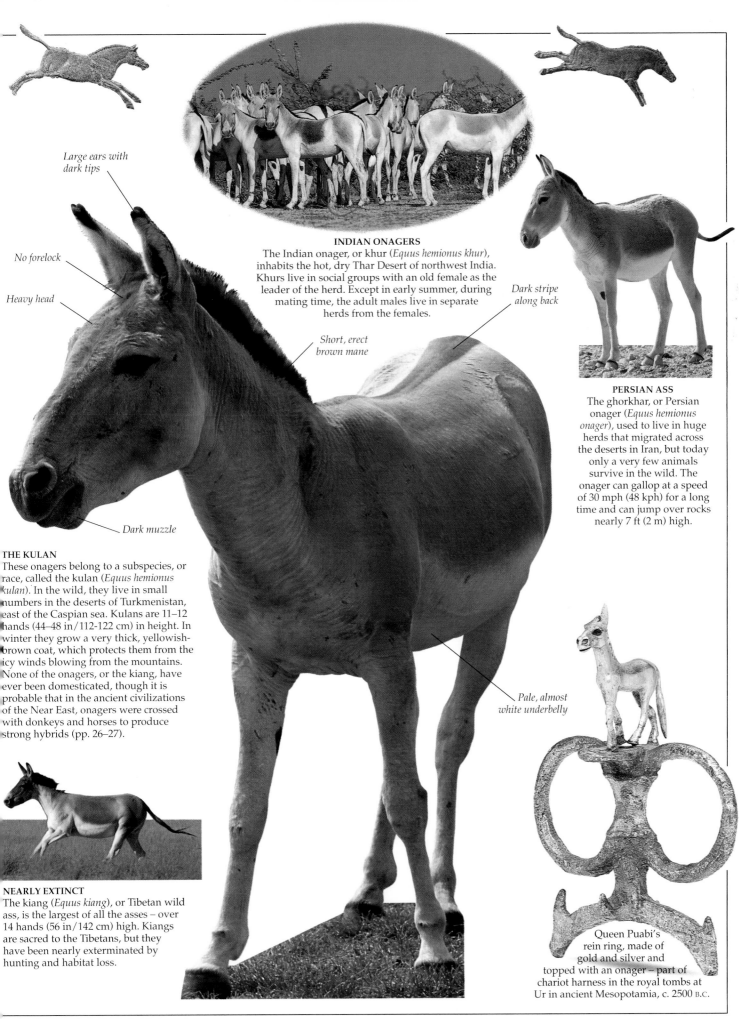

Large ears with
dark tips

No forelock

Heavy head

Dark muzzle

INDIAN ONAGERS
The Indian onager, or khur (*Equus hemionus khur*),
inhabits the hot, dry Thar Desert of northwest India.
Khurs live in social groups with an old female as the
leader of the herd. Except in early summer, during
mating time, the adult males live in separate
herds from the females.

Dark stripe
along back

Short, erect
brown mane

PERSIAN ASS
The ghorkhar, or Persian
onager (*Equus hemionus
onager*), used to live in huge
herds that migrated across
the deserts in Iran, but today
only a very few animals
survive in the wild. The
onager can gallop at a speed
of 30 mph (48 kph) for a long
time and can jump over rocks
nearly 7 ft (2 m) high.

THE KULAN
These onagers belong to a subspecies, or
race, called the kulan (*Equus hemionus
kulan*). In the wild, they live in small
numbers in the deserts of Turkmenistan,
east of the Caspian sea. Kulans are 11–12
hands (44–48 in/112-122 cm) in height. In
winter they grow a very thick, yellowish-
brown coat, which protects them from the
icy winds blowing from the mountains.
None of the onagers, or the kiang, have
ever been domesticated, though it is
probable that in the ancient civilizations
of the Near East, onagers were crossed
with donkeys and horses to produce
strong hybrids (pp. 26–27).

Pale, almost
white underbelly

NEARLY EXTINCT
The kiang (*Equus kiang*), or Tibetan wild
ass, is the largest of all the asses – over
14 hands (56 in/142 cm) high. Kiangs
are sacred to the Tibetans, but they
have been nearly exterminated by
hunting and habitat loss.

Queen Puabi's
rein ring, made of
gold and silver and
topped with an onager – part of
chariot harness in the royal tombs at
Ur in ancient Mesopotamia, c. 2500 B.C.

Seeing stripes

Large, rounded ears

TODAY, ZEBRAS LIVE ONLY IN AFRICA, though their ancestors, like all other members of the horse family, evolved in North America. There are three living species of zebra – Grévy's, common, and mountain. Each is found in different habitats and each has different patterns of stripes. The quagga, a fourth species, which used to live in the colder climate of Africa's southern tip but was exterminated by hunters by the late 1800s, had a thicker coat than most surviving species and fewer stripes on its body. Zebras feed on coarse grasses and travel over huge areas as they graze. They are very social and spend much time grooming – nuzzling each other's manes and withers with their front teeth. Zebras live in family groups in herds of up to a hundred or more. It is not known why zebras are striped, but the stripes may serve as camouflage through the mirages caused by heat waves – a solid-colored animal would show up better. Zebras will also stand tightly together and defend themselves and their young with their hooves and teeth.

White ears with black tips

BIG EARS
The Grévy's large, round ears are used to signal other individuals as well as to listen for sounds over great distances in its semidesert habitat.

Oval ears

Very dark muzzle

Small, squarish dewlap on throat

Thinner stripes down legs

No stripes on belly

Stripes of backbone go down tail

Broad, well-marked stripes over rump

Shadows between stripes

Donkey-like tail, with hair only at its tip

Seven-year-old female mountain zebra

Six-year-old common or plains zebra mare and her three-month-old foal

MOUNTAIN ZEBRA
The mountain zebra (*Equus zebra*) is now an endangered species that may soon be extinct like the quagga. It is found in small numbers in the mountain ranges of the western Cape province of South Africa and up the west coast to Angola. Like the common zebra, the mountain zebra averages around 13 hands (52 in/132 cm) at the withers.

ZEBROID
Zebras can inter-breed with all other horse species, but their offspring are infertile, like the mule (pp. 26–27). The animal (shown here) is a cross, or hybrid, between a zebra and a horse.

COMMON STRIPES
The common zebra (*Equus burchelli*), at around 13 hands (52 in/132 cm), once ranged throughout eastern and southern Africa, from Sudan to the Cape. Today, it is still widespread, and herds can be seen in almost all wildlife reserves. Young males live in bachelor groups until they can form their own families. Zebras are very social – if one member of the group is missing, they will search for it.

Dorsal or back stripe is broad and black

Very narrow stripes on face

GRÉVY'S ZEBRA
Grévy's zebra (*Equus grevyi*) is the most northern of the species and lives in small numbers in the semidesert areas of Kenya, Ethiopia, and Somalia. It is the largest of the zebras, with an average height of 14–15 hands (56–60 in/142–152 cm). It is not closely related to the other zebras and is considered to be a more primitive member of the horse family.

Rounded ears

No forelock

V-shaped brown patch on nose

Very tall, erect mane

White on either side of black dorsal stripe

Narrow, closely spaced black stripes on a white background, especially over the withers

White underbelly

Two female Grévy's zebras, age three to four years

Broad hooves

Stripes go down legs, ending in black coronet, above hoof

Pale-brown shadow striping between black stripes

Black dorsal stripe becomes thinner down the tail, with stripes on either side

Stripes bend around, becoming horizontal over haunches, not vertical

White inside of leg with no stripes

THE HORSELIKE QUAGGA
Early explorers in southern Africa found herds of more than 100 quaggas (*Equus quagga*) on their yearly migrations to different grazing grounds. Gradually, they were reduced in number by indiscriminate hunting; the last wild quaggas were shot in 1861. A few survived in zoos until the last one died in Amsterdam in the Netherlands in 1883.

ZEDONK
Another type of crossbreeding – between a zebra and a donkey – can result in pale-brown-colored animals with very fine stripes, such as these zedonks from Zimbabwe in south-central Africa. Many zoos around the world carry out successful crossbreeding programs.

Ancient ancestors

Fossil evidence tells us that at the end of the last ice age, 10,000 years ago (pp. 8–9), there must have been millions of horses living wild all over Europe and in northern and central Asia. These animals belonged to one species, called *Equus ferus*, that roamed in herds over the grasslands and probably migrated for hundreds of miles each year. As the climate changed, the grasslands were replaced by forests. The horses dwindled in number from loss of their habitat (area in which they lived) and from extensive hunting by humans. By 4,000 years ago very few wild horses were left in Europe, though two sub-species of wild horse – in Russia, the tarpan (*Equus ferus ferus*), and in Mongolia, Przewalski's horse (*Equus ferus przewalskii*) – survived until relatively recently. Also around 4,000 years ago, the first wild horses were being tamed and domesticated in eastern Europe, and they soon spread westward (pp. 22–23). All the domestic horses in the world today are descended from these domesticated ancestors, and they are classified in one species, called *Equus caballus*.

EXTINCT WILD HORSE
Many 18th-century travelers to the Russian steppes (plains) described herds of small wild horses, some of which were probably feral (pp. 32–33). The last tarpans died out in the early 1800s. In Poland today, ponies very like the tarpan have been re-created by breeding from primitive breeds such as the Konik.

Height range at withers of 13–14 hands (52–56 in/ 132–142 cm)

Short mane

Short forelock

AN ANCIENT ENGLISH PONY
The Exmoor pony is an ancient breed that closely resembles the extinct tarpan, or wild pony of eastern Europe. These ponies live in feral herds at Exmoor in southwest England.

Light-colored, flecked muzzle, typical of wild horse

SACRED WHITE HORSE
White horses were sacred animals to the Celts who lived in western Europe around 500 B.C. Around that time, this impression of a horse was scraped out from the white chalk hills at Whitehorse Hill in Berkshire, southern England.

Lumbar vertebra
Hipbone
Scapula
Cranium
Atlas or first cervical vertebra
Eye socket
Nasal bone
Axis
Lower jaw
Femur
Cervical vertebra
Upper cheek teeth
Coccygeal vertebra
Stifle joint
Rib
Humerus
Hock joint
Radius
Metacarpal bone
Knee
Metatarsal bone

SKELETON OF A PRZEWALSKI
The horse is built for speed. All its bones are long and slender, and they are attached to one another by ligaments, which are very strong and elastic so that the joints move easily. In the working horse (pp. 50–53), the framework of the skeleton is covered with powerful muscles and very little fat.

PRZEWALSKI HORSES
Wild horses were found living on the steppes of Mongolia by Russian travelers in the 1880s. A few were brought to Europe, where they bred in zoos and were later taken to America. Przewalski horses have been extinct in the wild since the 1960s, but now they are being reintroduced to Mongolia from herds bred in captivity.

Long, shaggy tail

Group of Przewalski horses

CAVE PAINTINGS
This wild horse (*Equus ferus*) was painted on a wall in the famous caves at Lascaux, France, by hunting people toward the end of the last ice age, about 14,000 years ago.

WILD AFRICAN ASS
The African wild ass (*Equus africanus*) is the ancestor of all domestic donkeys (pp. 24–25). It is still found in very small numbers in the eastern Sahara, but it is in danger of extinction.

Horses in history

T HE EARLIEST RELIABLE EVIDENCE for the domestication of the horse comes from the Ukraine, where people lived by herding horses and cattle on the grass steppes 6,000 years ago. At the same time, the African wild ass (pp. 16–17) was being domesticated in ancient Egypt and Arabia. At first horses and asses were not usually ridden but were harnessed in a pair to a cart or chariot. Soon the chariot became the status symbol of kings, who rode in them to battle, in royal parades, and for hunting. By the time of Homer, the Greek poet in the 8th century B.C., the riding of horses and donkeys had become a common means of travel (pp. 46–49), but chariots were still used for warfare (pp. 42–45). In the classical period of civilization, the ancient Greeks and Romans built special arenas and tracks for chariot races, which provided high drama for the crowds who watched these sporting events, involving riders, drivers, and horses (pp. 59–61).

THE END OF THE DAY
This horse's head from the Parthenon marbles (5th century B.C.) in Athens, Greece, is one of the greatest sculptures of all time. Legend has it that a team of horses would pull the Sun's chariot to the sea each day to create the sunset. The exhaustion from this extreme effort shows on the horse's face.

ROYAL STANDARD
This very early representation of donkeys harnessed to a four-wheeled cart is part of the mosaic decoration on a box – the Standard of Ur – from the royal tombs of Ur in ancient Mesopotamia (c. 2500 B.C.).

FLYING THROUGH THE AIR
Pegasus was a mythical horse with wings, who according to the ancient Greeks had sprung from the blood of Medusa when Perseus, a son of Zeus, cut off her head. The horse flew up to join the gods, but he was caught by Athena, the goddess of wisdom, and tamed with a golden bridle. This exquisite engraving of Pegasus is on a bronze cista, a container used to carry sacred utensils, made by the Etruscans, c. 300 B.C.

READY FOR WAR
This terra-cotta model from Cyprus probably represents an Assyrian warrior, 7th century B.C. The man carries a shield and is ready for battle. His horse has a breastplate and a warlike headdress.

HALF MAN, HALF HORSE
The myth of the centaurs – half men and half horses – may have arisen when people in ancient Greece saw the horsemen of Thessaly. Because they were unfamiliar with men on horseback, they believed they were seeing a new form of being. Shown here is a scene from the epic battles between the wild and lawless centaurs and the Lapiths of northern Greece, which appear in the magnificent sculptures in the Parthenon, 5th century B.C.

THE FOUR HORSES OF VENICE
Thought to be the work of 4th-century-B.C. Greek sculptor Lysippus, these magnificent bronze horses were taken from Constantinople (now Istanbul) in A.D. 1204 to the San Marco Basilica in Venice. Prior to this they had been in Rome. In 1797 Napoleon took the sculpture to Paris, and in 1815 the horses were returned to Venice.

BRAND MARK
Brands on horses (pp. 40–41) have been used as proof of ownership for more than 2,000 years. The hunting scene (above) is from a mosaic pavement (c. late 5th or 6th century B.C.) discovered at Carthage (a city founded by the Phoenicians near modern-day Tunis). The mosaic from North Africa shows a favorite pastime of wealthy landowners – hunting.

SURPRISE!
During the Trojan War, c. 1200 B.C., the Greeks invaded the city of Troy by hiding soldiers in a huge wood horse they had built. The Trojans, believing the Greeks had abandoned the horse, wheeled it into the city. Then the Greeks leaped out and opened the city gates to let in the conquering army.

A BIT OF A TANG
The people of China have always had a great respect for their horses. During the Tang dynasty (A.D. 618–907), many earthenware models of horses were produced that are of great artistic value today. The cobalt-blue glaze was very rare and expensive to produce at that time because cobalt was imported only in very small quantities. This figure would have been molded in several parts and then joined together as a whole.

Donkey work

THE DOMESTICATED ASS, OR DONKEY (*Equus asinus*), is descended from the African wild ass (*Equus africanus*, pp. 16–17), which survives today in very small numbers in the hot, dry deserts of North Africa. Because of this harsh environment, the donkey has developed great strength, stamina, and endurance to carry heavy loads over long distances on little food and water. In the wild, donkey foals have to develop quickly so that they can keep up with the herd as it travels great distances in search of edible bushes and grass. Female donkeys, or jennies, carry their foals for 12 months before they are born – a gestation period of one month longer than the female horse's (pp. 14–15). In the desert and on rocky ground the donkey's small, neat hooves are kept evenly worn down, but they will grow and must be filed if the animal is kept on soft grass. Like all members of the horse family, the donkey is a social animal and needs to live with other animals if it is to thrive.

JESUS ON A DONKEY
When Jesus was born, the donkey was the usual means of transportation in Jerusalem, which is why the baby Jesus is always portrayed with his mother on a donkey, led by Joseph. The "cross" on a donkey's back – a dark stripe along the backbone and a horizontal band across the shoulders – combined with the fact that Jesus rode a donkey on the first Palm Sunday made people believe that these hairs had healing powers.

ANDALUSIAN GOATHERD
In Andalusia, in southwestern Spain, donkeys are still used for herding and farmwork. This family is traveling by donkey to take their goats to new pastures.

Rein

Breeching (straps that go under animal's haunches)

GREEK HARVEST
Until recently in Greece, it was a common sight to see donkeys threshing grain. By walking around and around in a circle, the donkeys' hooves separate the seeds from the husks.

WATER, WATER
Water is the most precious of all resources in desert countries, and it often has to be fetched from far away. This North African woman from Tunisia is carrying her baby and leading her donkey, loaded with water jars.

Wooden shaft

Foot stand for stepping up into cart

Mid-19th-century English donkey cart

Long ears help donkey keep cool

Lighter juvenile coat on back

Darker adult coat, like his father's, now visible at first shedding

Typical white muzzle

POITOU DONKEYS

For hundreds of years in Spain and in the Poitou region of France, there has been a tradition of breeding very large donkeys, which are used to mate with female horses to produce giant mules (pp. 26–27) for farmwork, in the same way cart horses were used in more northern countries. Poitou donkeys stand about 14 hands (56 in/ 142 cm) at the shoulder, or withers, making them the world's largest donkeys. They also have very long, dark, shaggy coats.

White underbelly

Long, slender legs

A family group: five-year-old father, nine-year-old mother, and eleven-month-old son

This poor old donkey has had a hard working life and now deserves a peaceful retirement

AFRICAN DONKEYS

These donkeys are drinking from a water hole in Kenya, where they are living semiwild on a ranch. They must fend for themselves and learn to keep away from leopards, hyenas, and other predators, just as other wild animals have to do.

Hame

Rein ring

Bridle

Decorated browband

Blinker

Noseband

Bit

Collar

Trace

Girth

Ten-year-old Irish donkey, at 11.2 hands (46 in/ 117 cm)

DONKEYS OF IRELAND

Donkeys are the traditional pack and work animals of Ireland, one of the few countries in northern Europe where they have been bred for hundreds of years and have become adapted to a climate that is very different from the deserts where they evolved. Irish donkeys have much shorter legs than the donkeys from the hotter Mediterranean and Arabian regions, and they have much thicker coats so they can survive the cold.

Long ears

Long tail, with tuft at tip

Well-trimmed hooves

REGAL WHITE DONKEYS

Donkeys are now popular as pets for children and on farms. This has led to breeding for new looks, like these white donkeys with curly coats. In the ancient world white donkeys were the favored mounts of royalty.

Mules and hinnies

Breast collar (easier to fit than larger collar, as chest is so narrow)

Long, asslike ears of its father

THE SUMERIANS OF MESOPOTAMIA were the first people to inter-breed horses and donkeys to produce mules (donkey father, horse mother) and hinnies (horse father, donkey mother) about 4,000 years ago. Records of Roman agriculture tell how the donkey stallions kept for mule breeding were brought up with horses so that they would mate more readily with the mares. For thousands of years mules have been used as pack animals (pp. 46–47) to carry huge loads, because they combine the donkey's stamina with the horse's strength. Like its parents, a mule is a herd animal that travels best in a "mule train" (a long line of mules harnessed together to pull loads). A "bell mare" (a specially trained female horse with a bell around her neck) would lead the mules, who learned to follow the bell's sound, so they could travel at night without being lost in the dark. The horse family is unusual in that all the species can interbreed. However, although the resulting offspring will grow to be healthy animals, they are sterile and cannot breed.

During a hard day's travel, a working mule feeds from a nose bag filled with oats

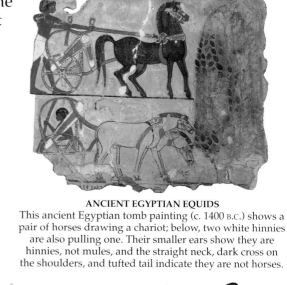

ANCIENT EGYPTIAN EQUIDS
This ancient Egyptian tomb painting (c. 1400 B.C.) shows a pair of horses drawing a chariot; below, two white hinnies are also pulling one. Their smaller ears show they are hinnies, not mules, and the straight neck, dark cross on the shoulders, and tufted tail indicate they are not horses.

Crate of ducks

INDIAN TRAVEL
Mule carts are still used in Asia and have remained unchanged for at least 3,000 years. However, the method of harnessing has changed, for the earliest carts were always attached to a pair of mules or horses with a central wood pole. The idea of putting a single animal between two wood shafts was not invented until 2,000 years ago. Here the mule has a bridle with a bit, and it is driven with reins. All the family's goods are piled into the cart, including their ducks.

14-year-old mule, 13.3 hands (55 in/140 cm), drawing Indian cart (c. 1840)

A POWERFUL MULE
Mules travel faster than oxen and are more surefooted than horses over difficult terrain, so 19th-century settlers preferred these animals for hauling huge loads over bad muddy roads on their long trek west across North America (pp. 34–35). Mules were also used underground in mines and as pack animals in wartime.

Large body

Heavy head with long ears

Neat front legs

Strong hind legs

Long tail, like a horse

TOURIST CLASS
People will always enjoy a leisurely drive in a carriage, and even in the busy streets of New Orleans, as in most large cities, a carriage ride is still possible. This mule, hitched to a post decorated with a horse's head, waits patiently to give its next ride around town to the tourists.

No forelock, like a donkey (pp. 24–25)

Short ears

Typical short donkey-like mane

Crossbreeding

When a donkey is crossed with a horse, the foal has what is called "hybrid vigor" – that is, it is stronger and healthier than either of its parents. The most common crossbreed is a donkey stallion (or jackass) with a horse mare, which produces a mule, but if a horse stallion is crossed with a female donkey (or jenny) the hybrid offspring is called a hinny (or jennet). Generally, a mule is a stronger animal than a hinny.

STUBBORN AS A HINNY
This eight-year old white hinny (whose parents were a female donkey and a pony stallion) will not be pulled where it does not want to go. Donkeys (pp. 24–25), mules, and hinnies all have a reputation for being stubborn, but this is because their natural behavioral patterns are not understood correctly. They are herd animals, they are intelligent, and they are nervous of going to a new place on their own. Once they are trained to follow a person or a bell mare, they will go anywhere, even to places of great danger.

Mule misbehaves (pp. 12–13)

Dark gray spots on white, shorthaired coat

Long, tufted tail, used for swishing flies or to show it is anxious

Eight-year-old hinny

27

Shoes and shoeing

THE HOOVES OF ALL EQUIDS are made from keratin, a protein that is the same organic (natural) substance as hair or human fingernails. Just like hair and nails, the hooves can be cut and shaped without discomfort to the animal. The hooves of a domestic horse wear down evenly if it is ridden over flat, hard ground, but if the land is rocky, the hooves may split and chip. If the ground is muddy and soft, the hooves may grow too long and become diseased. It is necessary, therefore, for the horse to have regular attention from a blacksmith, a person specially trained to look after hooves and fit them with metal shoes for protection. The hoof is made up of three parts – the wall, or outer part, to which the shoe is attached with nails; the sole; and the frog, the wedge-shaped part at the center.

Old horseshoe and nails just removed from horse's hoof by blacksmith

1 REMOVE OLD SHOE
The horse stands patiently while the blacksmith cuts off the old nails and removes the old shoe.

INDIAN SHOES
The methods of shoeing horses have been much the same all over the world for hundreds of years. Here three workers, surrounded by all their equipment, are shoeing a fine horse during the time of the Mogul emperors in northern India, c. A.D. 1600.

Girth's powerful muscles enable horse to do very heavy work (pp. 50–53)

Feathering on foot

Blacksmith's box of essential tools for shoeing horses

Shoeing a four-year-old Shire horse

GAME OF LUCK
All over the world, the horseshoe is a talisman for good luck. It must always be held with the open part at the top so that the good luck will not drop out. Horseshoe pitching – a game based on luck – is a popular pastime in the U.S. and Canada. Shown here is an iron horseshoe (c. 1st century A.D.), found in southern England.

Horseshoe-shaped growth, removed by blacksmith along with old shoe

2 CLEANING THE HOOF
The worn layer of the sole is clipped off, the new layer is filed down, and the whole hoof is cleaned and made ready for the new shoe.

3 SHAPING UP
The new iron shoe for the hoof is made red hot in the furnace at 2,000°F (1,090°C). Using a heavy hammer, the blacksmith shapes the shoe on his anvil.

4 STEAMING
After the shoe has been reheated, it is pressed onto the hoof to check the fit and then allowed to cool. The hoof gives off a smell of burning hair and much smoke, but this does not hurt the horse.

Height at withers 17.2 hands (70 in/ 178 cm)

Chestnut

6 FINISHED FOOT
The rim of the foot is then filed, as is the hoof just under the nail ends, before the blacksmith hammers them flat. The nails should be flush with the shoe, and the hoof and the outside edge of the shoe should match precisely.

Filing hoof and nail ends flat

Balancing on one front foot

5 NAILING ON THE SHOE
Then the blacksmith takes some special iron nails and hammers them through the predrilled holes in the shoe. The nail ends that show through the horse's hoof are cut off and bent back.

WHEN "HIPPO" MEANT "HORSE"
Iron horseshoes were invented after the Roman period, but the Romans often tied a shoe made of wicker or metal onto the hoof with leather straps. This was called a "hipposandal," from the Greek *hippo* meaning "horse."

Hipposandal, French, 1st–3rd century A.D.

Bits and pieces

Back view of woman riding sidesaddle

JINGLE BELLS
Bells on the harness were a safety feature. If horses and passengers became lost in snow-covered countryside, the bells' chimes would let rescuers know their position.

THE EARLIEST DOMESTIC horses and asses were probably ridden bareback and guided by a rope that was tied around the lower jaw in the gap between the cheek teeth and the incisors. Today this remains a common way of controlling donkeys in Turkey and Greece. The first bits, or mouthpieces of the bridle, were made of hide, bone, or wood and had fastenings at each end to which reins were attached. Beginning c. 1500 B.C. bits were made of bronze, and later iron. Until late Roman times, riders did not use saddles – they rode bareback or on a horse cloth – and there were no stirrups (loops suspended from a horse's saddle to support rider's foot) in Europe until the 8th century A.D. The lack of saddles and stirrups did not prevent either Eurasian riders, or later, Native Americans (pp. 56–57) from holding their bows and shooting arrows from a galloping horse. The most powerful nomadic horse riders in the ancient world were the Scythians (pp. 32–33) from central Asia in the 5th and 4th centuries B.C. They had very elaborate harnesses, but they still rode with only a single saddle cloth and no stirrups. These horses were the riders' most valuable possessions and were buried with them in their tombs.

SPURRED ON
The horses of the Middle Ages in 13th-century Europe had a very hard time, for they were bridled with bits and goaded by armored knights wearing cruel spurs (U-shaped devices attached to heel of rider's boot, pp. 44–45). These were either prickspurs or rowel spurs with little wheels.

Rowel spur (9.1 in/23 cm), made of iron and brass, western Europe, early 1500s

Rowel

Screw would have clamped stirrup to outside of shoe

Metal part of stirrup would have fitted inside heel of shoe

Tiny rowel spur (1.6 in/4 cm), made of iron and fitting directly onto shoe, Europe, late 1600s

Buckle for attaching stirrup to boot

Metal part of stirrup for "pricking" horse

Prickspur (11.4 in/29 cm), made of iron, N.W. Africa (Moorish), early 1800s

PUTTING YOUR FOOT IN IT
It is thought that the Chinese invented metal foot stirrups in the 5th century A.D. Stirrups then spread slowly westward to Europe. The use of stirrups altered the way battles were fought (pp. 44–45), because they allowed riders to wield their weapons without falling off.

Iron stirrup, Bulgaria, A.D. 800–900

Decorated boot stirrup, made of iron, Spain, 1600s

Brass fretwork

Box stirrup, made of painted wood and brass fretwork, France or Italy, late 1700s

Dragon decoration

Brass stirrup, decorated with two dragons, China, 1800s

Joint

Rein ring

Jointed snaffle bit,
Ireland, 100 B.C.–A.D. 100

BUILD A BETTER BIT
Three types of bit have been invented for
controlling domesticated horses. The first
is the simple, straight "snaffle" bit, which
developed into a jointed mouthpiece in
Assyria, c. 900 B.C. The "curb" bit is a
straight bit with a chain fixed under the
horse's chin, acting as a lever and pulling
on its mouth. The third bit is the
"pelham" – a combination of a snaffle
and curb bit with double reins.

Detail from the Bayeux tapestry from France, c. 1080

DEFEAT IN BATTLE
In the Battle of Hastings, 1066, the 7,000
troops brought over from Normandy
by William the Conqueror fought
against the English. One reason
why they won the war was that
they fought on horseback with the
new invention of stirrups, while
the English dismounted and
fought in the old way on foot.

Joint

Rein ring

Cheekpiece

Jointed snaffle
bit with cheekpiece,
Bulgaria, A.D. 800–900

Curb chain

**Double rollers in
horse's mouth**

Rein ring

Brass boss

Curb bit (length 12 in/305 mm, width 2 in/50
mm), made of steel and brass, Europe, 1500s

Brass boss

Rein ring

Curb chain

Mouthpiece

Curb bit (length 7.3 in/185 mm,
width 4.3 in/110 mm),
made of steel and brass,
Portugal, 1800s

Brow-band

Crownpiece

Throatlatch

*Height at withers 17 hands
(68 in/173 cm)*

Rein

Bit

RIDING SIDESADDLE
This gray Lipizzaner mare
is being ridden sidesaddle.
Women today usually ride
like this only when they are
competing in a dressage
event (pp. 60–61). In former
times, from the early 1300s
onward, the sidesaddle was
the only way a female rider,
wearing long, heavy skirts,
could be mounted on a
horse. Many women found
it a very comfortable way
of riding.

Girth

Stirrup

*Rider on leather
saddle made-to-
measure in 1890*

Woman, in Victorian dress, riding
sidesaddle on a six-year-old Lipizzaner

Rein ring (terret),
England,
1st century A.D.

Strap-union made of bronze
(for joining straps together),
England, 1st century A.D.

Decorated terret
(a ring on saddle
harness through
which driving
reins pass), found in
Egypt, 1st century B.C.

Exploring by horse

WITHOUT THE HORSE AND THE ASS, human history would have been quite different. Civilizations would have evolved in their places of origin, and their peoples would not have traveled around the world in quest of new places to explore and conquer. There would have been no Crusades, and Europeans could not have destroyed the indigenous cultures of the Americas. An invading force has to have fast transportation and an efficient way to move goods, weapons, and food; otherwise it is powerless against the defenses of settled communities. Although horse riding was the general means of transportation from at least 1000 B.C., it was not until 2,000 years later, in the 11th century A.D., that horses were commonly shod and a saddle and stirrups generally used. From this time onward, the horse became increasingly important in war and sport (pp. 42–45), and great travelers like Marco Polo could ride huge distances across Europe and Asia – journeys that today would be considered long even by airplane.

VIKING CHESSMAN
This knight on horseback, carved from a walrus tusk during the 12th century, is one of the famous chessmen found on the Isle of Lewis off Scotland's west coast.

GENGHIS KHAN
Genghis Khan (A.D. 1162–1227), the Mongolian conqueror, ruled an empire of nomadic horsemen that stretched across Asia into Europe – from the Pacific Ocean to the Black Sea.

Pair of bronze Etruscan riders, c. 500 B.C.

ARCHERS OF THE ANCIENT WORLD
These two elegant Etruscan bronzes from northern Italy, c. 500 B.C., show how – even without saddle and stirrups – Scythian archers could shoot their arrows from a galloping horse. The archer shooting backward exemplifies the "Parthian shot," a technique commonly used by the nomadic horsemen on the steppes of central Asia.

Statue of Charlemagne, the Holy Roman Emperor

HOLY ROMAN EMPEROR
Charlemagne, or Charles the Great (A.D. 742–814), was the most famous ruler of the Middle Ages. As emperor of the Frankish kingdom, he conquered Saxony and Lombardy. In A.D. 796 he led over 15,000 horsemen against the Avars in Hungary. In A.D. 800 he was crowned Emperor of the Holy Roman Empire, stretching from Denmark to central Italy, from France to Austria.

Fretwork

IN THE SADDLE
This 18th-century Tibetan wood saddle, decorated with gold and silver fretwork, may have been similar to one owned by Genghis Khan 600 years earlier.

Tree

Cantle

Pommel

18th-century Tibetan saddle

ALEXANDER THE GREAT
Bucephalus, a black stallion born c. 331 B.C., is probably the most famous horse to have ever lived. He belonged to Alexander the Great (356–323 B.C.), who was 20 when he became the king of Macedon. Together they conquered the world – from Greece in the west to Egypt in the south, and as far east as India.

Stone frieze of Alexander the Great on his horse, Bucephalus (left), on a sarcophagus in Syria

PATRON SAINT OF ENGLAND AND PORTUGAL
This icon of St. George, who is believed to have died in A.D. 303, was made by a 13th-century crusader.

Archer showing "Parthian shot"

Tassel on bridle

Curb ring

Curb chain

Gold embroidery on felt, stitched onto leather backing

GOLDEN WONDER
This exquisite gold model of a four-horse chariot, c. 5th century B.C., is from the Achaemenid empire of Persia (now Iran). It is unusual in that it has two poles to which the two pairs of horses are harnessed.

Part of treasure found near the Oxus River in central Asia

Reins

Early-19th-century North African bridle with curb bit

To the Americas

Before 1492, when the first European settlers arrived in both North and South America, the continents were densely populated with native peoples, who had arrived there between 20,000 and 10,000 years earlier. The European invaders had a fast means of transportation for people and supplies – the horse and the mule.

FINE HATS
For ceremonial occasions the Sioux chieftains, from America's northern plains, wear their finest headdresses, made of wild turkey feathers, and ride their most beautiful horses.

Therefore, they were able to conquer the Native Americans and take over vast areas of land. Soon a few horses escaped to live and breed in the wild. Within a hundred years they had spread over all the grasslands (pp. 36–37). The Native Americans of both continents quickly realized the value of the horse. By bartering with the Spanish, they obtained their own stock, which they learned to ride with as much dexterity as the ancient Scythians, who could shoot an arrow from a bow while riding a galloping horse without stirrups (pp. 32–33).

THE BLACK HAWK WAR
Like other North American tribes, the Sauk Indians of the northern Mississippi River used horses for transportation, hunting, and fighting wars. Keokuk (c. 1760–1848, above), was appointed Sauk chief by American officials and signed treaties giving away much of the Sauk land. Black Hawk, the Sauks' true leader, and his people fiercely defended their land but in the end were defeated. By 1840, millions of acres of Indian territory were ceded to the whites.

Blaze

Central wood shaft, or "tongue," to which harness is attached

BEASTS OF BURDEN
Before there were railroads across the North American continent, teams of six or more mules (pp. 26–27) would haul heavily laden wagons along roads that were often deep in mud and impassable by any other means of transportation.

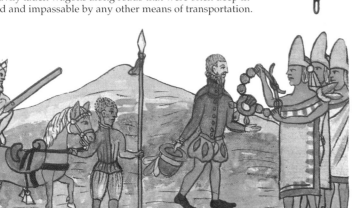

Martingale

Stocking

DOWN MEXICO WAY
In the early 1500s, Spanish conquistadores brought horses (similar to Andalusians, pp. 40–41) to the New World, where they had been extinct for 10,000 years. Here Indians present Hernando Cortés (1485–1547), the conqueror of Mexico, with a treasured necklace.

Shod hoof, giving better grip in soft earth

WESTWARD, HO!
Trappers, traders, and missionaries were the first to reach the Pacific, but in 1843 a determined band of 1,000 settlers left Missouri on the 2,000-mile (3,300-km) trek westward along the Oregon Trail. To protect themselves from attack, they would form their wagons into a circle at dusk. Finally after many grueling months, bad weather, disease, poor food, and crossing the Rocky Mountains, they reached their destination.

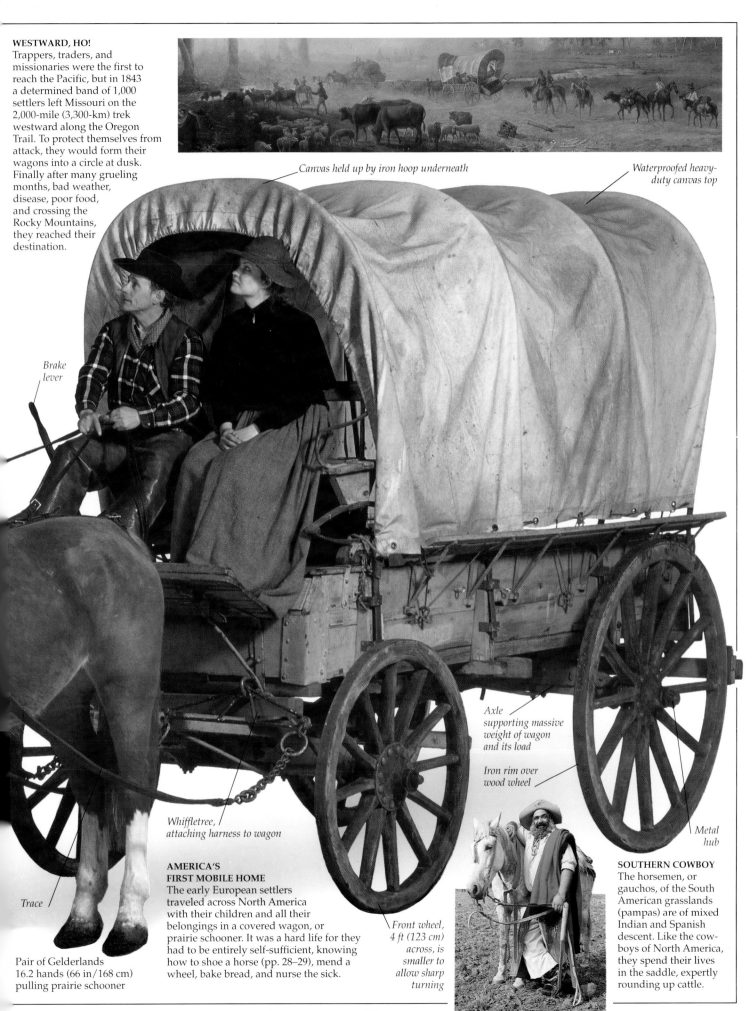

Canvas held up by iron hoop underneath

Waterproofed heavy-duty canvas top

Brake lever

Axle supporting massive weight of wagon and its load

Iron rim over wood wheel

Metal hub

Whiffletree, attaching harness to wagon

Trace

Pair of Gelderlands 16.2 hands (66 in/168 cm) pulling prairie schooner

AMERICA'S FIRST MOBILE HOME
The early European settlers traveled across North America with their children and all their belongings in a covered wagon, or prairie schooner. It was a hard life for they had to be entirely self-sufficient, knowing how to shoe a horse (pp. 28–29), mend a wheel, bake bread, and nurse the sick.

Front wheel, 4 ft (123 cm) across, is smaller to allow sharp turning

SOUTHERN COWBOY
The horsemen, or gauchos, of the South American grasslands (pampas) are of mixed Indian and Spanish descent. Like the cowboys of North America, they spend their lives in the saddle, expertly rounding up cattle.

Running wild

THERE ARE NO LONGER ANY TRULY WILD HORSES living in the wild, but all over the world there are many herds of horses and ponies that are considered "feral." Feral animals are descended from domesticated (tamed) stock but are no longer under human control, and they live and breed in the wild. The last truly wild horses were the Przewalski horses (pp. 20–21), which survived in small numbers on the Mongolian steppes (plains) until the 1960s. At the end of the 15th century, horses spread rapidly over the grasslands of North and South America soon after the first Europeans arrived (pp. 34–35), bringing their mounts with them. Soon there were millions of horses living wild. Today, the number of feral horses – for example, the mustang of North America and the Australian brumby – is much less than in the past. The population is controlled – some are killed by hunters, and others are rounded up and domesticated.

FELL PONIES
In Britain there are many breeds of pony that live on the moors, like the Fell pony. Although Fell ponies are domesticated, they are allowed to live and breed with very little human control. Traditionally, Fell ponies have been used as pack ponies, for riding, and for light draft work.

Long ears

Well-proportioned head

Coat colors vary from bay, brown, and gray, but never piebald or skewbald (pp. 38–41)

GERMAN DÜLMEN
These rare ponies live semiwild on the Duke of Croy's estate in Westphalia, Germany. They have been crossbred with both British and Polish ponies, so they are not purebred. The herd dates back to the early 1300s.

Strong legs support sturdy, well-built body

Strong horny hooves

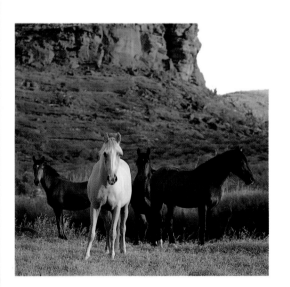

THE BRUMBY OF AUSTRALIA
For 150 years there have been herds of feral horses in Australia, ever since they were abandoned during the gold rush. These horses, called brumbies, formed herds and reproduced in great numbers over large areas. They are unpopular with cattle and sheep ranchers because they compete for grazing and usually carry many parasites. Since the 1960s, they have been hunted so extensively that there are now very few.

SYMBOLIC HORSES
A wild running horse has often been used as a symbol of freedom and elegance. It has advertised many things, from banks to sports cars – such as the Mustang and Pinto in the U.S. and (as shown here) the Ferrari, the supreme speedster.

THE MUSTANGS OF AMERICA
The feral horses, or mustangs, of the Nevada desert have hard lives traveling great distances in search of enough grass and water to live on.

DAWN IN THE CAMARGUE
The beautiful white horses from the Camargue in the south of France have lived wild in the marshes of the Rhone delta for over a thousand years. They have very wide hooves for living on soft wet grassland.

Star

Short stripe on face

Long, straight, full mane

Snip

Deep girth

Full forelock

Blaze

New Forest ponies range in height from 12.2 to 14.2 hands (127–147 cm)

THE PONIES OF THE NEW FOREST
In Britain there have been herds of ponies living in the New Forest woodlands of Hampshire, England, since the 11th century. For 700 years these ponies lived wild there, but in the 18th and 19th centuries attempts were made to increase their size by bringing in stallions of other breeds. They still run wild in their native area, but also are reared on private stud farms to provide ideal ponies for children and adults to ride and for light draft work (pp. 54–55).

Horses from around the world

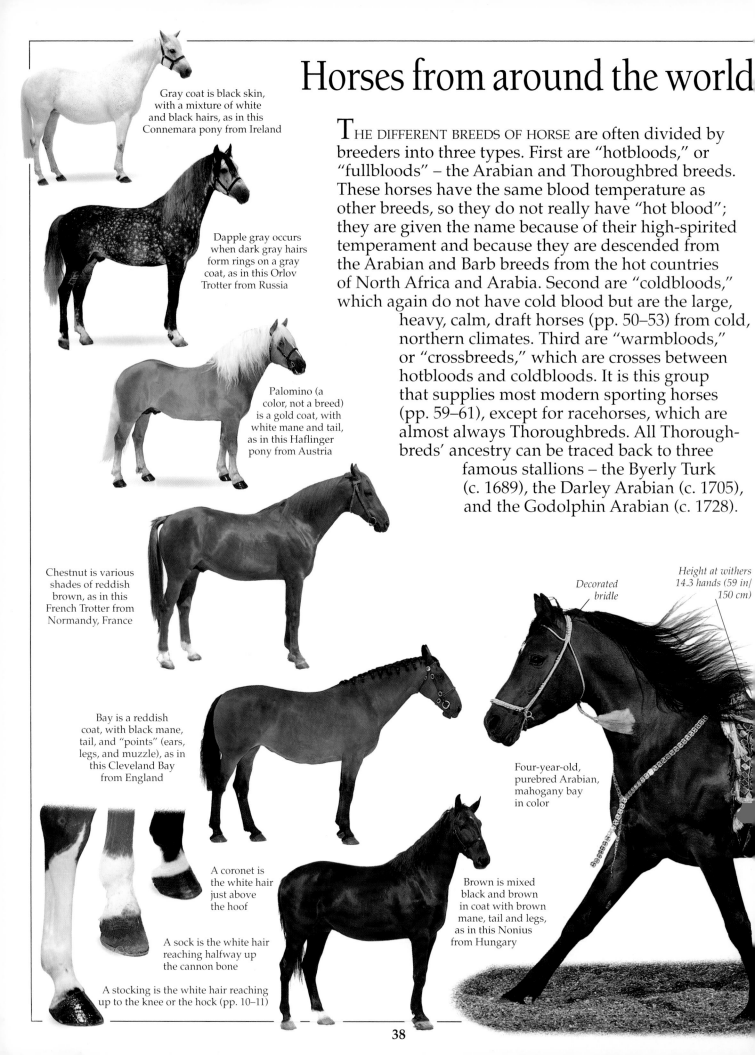

T HE DIFFERENT BREEDS OF HORSE are often divided by breeders into three types. First are "hotbloods," or "fullbloods" – the Arabian and Thoroughbred breeds. These horses have the same blood temperature as other breeds, so they do not really have "hot blood"; they are given the name because of their high-spirited temperament and because they are descended from the Arabian and Barb breeds from the hot countries of North Africa and Arabia. Second are "coldbloods," which again do not have cold blood but are the large, heavy, calm, draft horses (pp. 50–53) from cold, northern climates. Third are "warmbloods," or "crossbreeds," which are crosses between hotbloods and coldbloods. It is this group that supplies most modern sporting horses (pp. 59–61), except for racehorses, which are almost always Thoroughbreds. All Thorough-breds' ancestry can be traced back to three famous stallions – the Byerly Turk (c. 1689), the Darley Arabian (c. 1705), and the Godolphin Arabian (c. 1728).

Gray coat is black skin, with a mixture of white and black hairs, as in this Connemara pony from Ireland

Dapple gray occurs when dark gray hairs form rings on a gray coat, as in this Orlov Trotter from Russia

Palomino (a color, not a breed) is a gold coat, with white mane and tail, as in this Haflinger pony from Austria

Chestnut is various shades of reddish brown, as in this French Trotter from Normandy, France

Bay is a reddish coat, with black mane, tail, and "points" (ears, legs, and muzzle), as in this Cleveland Bay from England

Decorated bridle

Height at withers 14.3 hands (59 in/ 150 cm)

Four-year-old, purebred Arabian, mahogany bay in color

A coronet is the white hair just above the hoof

A sock is the white hair reaching halfway up the cannon bone

A stocking is the white hair reaching up to the knee or the hock (pp. 10–11)

Brown is mixed black and brown in coat with brown mane, tail and legs, as in this Nonius from Hungary

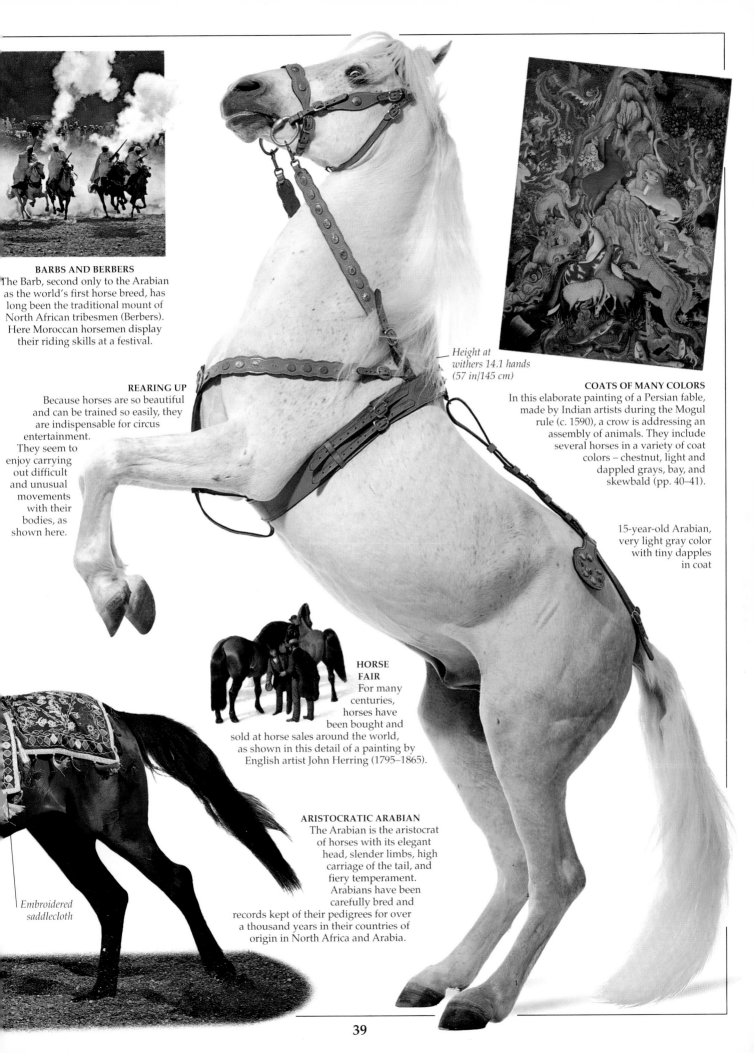

BARBS AND BERBERS
The Barb, second only to the Arabian as the world's first horse breed, has long been the traditional mount of North African tribesmen (Berbers). Here Moroccan horsemen display their riding skills at a festival.

REARING UP
Because horses are so beautiful and can be trained so easily, they are indispensable for circus entertainment. They seem to enjoy carrying out difficult and unusual movements with their bodies, as shown here.

Height at withers 14.1 hands (57 in/145 cm)

COATS OF MANY COLORS
In this elaborate painting of a Persian fable, made by Indian artists during the Mogul rule (c. 1590), a crow is addressing an assembly of animals. They include several horses in a variety of coat colors – chestnut, light and dappled grays, bay, and skewbald (pp. 40–41).

15-year-old Arabian, very light gray color with tiny dapples in coat

HORSE FAIR
For many centuries, horses have been bought and sold at horse sales around the world, as shown in this detail of a painting by English artist John Herring (1795–1865).

Embroidered saddlecloth

ARISTOCRATIC ARABIAN
The Arabian is the aristocrat of horses with its elegant head, slender limbs, high carriage of the tail, and fiery temperament. Arabians have been carefully bred and records kept of their pedigrees for over a thousand years in their countries of origin in North Africa and Arabia.

More breeds and colors

EVERY COUNTRY HAS ITS OWN BREED OF HORSE – from the United States' Morgan horse, to southern Africa's Basuto pony, to Britain's Shire horse (pp. 50–53). Each breed is adapted to life in its place of origin, and each has its own uses. The breeds are defined by their "conformation," or size and body shape, as well as by their color and any white markings they may have on their faces and legs. Horses come in many different sizes – from the smallest horse in the world, the Falabella, which measures no more than 7.2 hands (30 in/76 cm) at the withers, to the largest of all breeds, the Shire horse. A Shire stallion should be 16.2 hands (66 in/168 cm) or higher and should weigh about one ton. Shires are usually brown or bay with a white blaze on their forehead. Their heavily feathered feet have white socks or stockings (pp. 38–39). In horse lore around the world, many sayings link a horse's behavior with its coat color. One Arab saying claims that all horses except bays are unlucky, unless they have some white markings. Another widespread belief of unknown origin is that chestnuts are fast but hot tempered.

Height at withers 16.1 hands (65 in/ 165 cm)

Flat metal stirrup

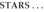

STARS . . .
It is usual for horses to have white markings on their faces, such as a regular or irregular star shape set high on the face between the eyes. An example is this Danish Warmblood, a breed now regarded as Denmark's national horse. A small white patch between the nostrils is called a snip.

. . . AND STRIPES
A long, narrow strip of white, extending from above the eyes to the nostrils, is called a stripe, as on this Oldenburg, a breed first established in Germany in the 1600s. A stripe can also be interrupted, with the coat color showing between the star, short stripe, and snip down the horse's face.

WHAT THE BLAZES!
A wide strip starting above the eyes and extending down to the muzzle is called a blaze, as on this Gelderland from the Netherlands, a breed that has existed for the last century. When white hair covers almost all the face from the forelock to the lips, it is called a bald face.

Seven-year-old dark gray purebred Andalusian ridden by a woman in classical Spanish riding costume

CLASSICAL EQUITATION
The Spanish Riding School was founded in 1572, when nine Lipizzaner stallions and 24 mares were brought to Vienna in Austria from Spain

HORSES IN ART

The beauty, elegance, and strength of the horse has fascinated sculptors and artists for thousands of years (pp. 22–23, 32–33). In this stylized work by the German painter Franz Marc (1880–1916) these horses have a very odd blue color to their coats.

THE "SPANISH HORSE"

Known as the "Spanish Horse" for centuries, Andalusian horses were first bred by Carthusian monks at three monasteries in southwest Spain at the end of the 1400s. The breed was possibly influenced by the Barbs of North Africa (pp. 38–39). Today the horses are usually gray, but they were originally chestnut or black.

Numnah (sheepskin pad to protect horse's back)

Spanish-style saddle blanket

Exhibiting spectacular Spanish walk, with one front and one rear leg raised in the air

Horses are called black when the coat, mane, tail, and legs are completely black, as in this beautiful Friesian from the Netherlands

Roan color can be either "red" (where the coat color is chestnut with white hairs mixed) or "blue" (a black or brown coat with a little white hair), as in this Italian Heavy Draft horse from Venice in northern Italy

Dun color can be a yellowish or gold coat (with black or other colors in the legs, mane, and tail), as in this Fjord pony from Norway. The dorsal stripe running along the mane and back into the tail is typical of this breed

A spotted coat can have five varieties of pattern, usually dark spots on light hair, as seen here in this little Falabella, first bred in Argentina

Skewbald refers to a coat with large patches of brown and white. This Pinto has a chestnut coat with white patches called overo (a dark coat with light patches); a white coat with colored patches is called tobiano

A piebald horse has large, irregular patches of white and black, as in this Shetland pony from the Scottish islands of the same name

41

War-horses

THE HORSE AND THE ASS have been used to assist humans in their wars of invasion for the last 5,000 years. By riding in chariots harnessed to a pair of horses, people could travel much faster than on foot and could cause much greater damage to the enemy. At first the "wars" were small squabbles between individuals, but then families grew larger and settled into villages, and battles sometimes took place between the villages. From the time of Alexander the Great (pp. 32–33), when armed horse riders (cavalry) developed, the horse played a major role in all wars until just after World War I, when mechanized vehicles took over. After stirrups became widespread in Europe in the early medieval period, the cavalry was better able to protect themselves and fight more efficiently because the stirrups and new, higher saddles gave a steadier seat; and riders were able to use longer weapons like lances. This meant that armor had to be heavier and horses had to be bred larger and stronger, but they were never as large as the heavy horses of today.

NAPOLEON'S FAVORITE CHARGER
Marengo was the white Arabian stallion ridden by the French leader Napoleon Bonaparte (1769–1821) during the Battle of Waterloo in Belgium in 1815 when he was defeated by the British. Although wounded during this battle, Marengo did not die until 1829.

Rider's uniform heavily embroidered with real gold thread

Made of pure silver, these drums weigh 150 lb (68 kg)

Royal coat of arms (featuring a lion and a unicorn) embroidered with real gold and silver threads on damask-silk drum banner

Double reins covered with real gold thread; boot reins connected to rider's stirrups, second set to rider's waist

Bridle's beard, or tassel, made of natural horse hair – black hair surrounding dyed red hair

TILTING AT WINDMILLS
In 1605 the Spanish poet Miguel Cervantes (1547–1616) created his most memorable character, Don Quixote, and his mount, Rosinante. He and his friend Sancho Panza (who rode a donkey) had all kinds of adventures, but their most famous one occurred when they used their lances to attack "giants" – which were really windmills.

THE DRUM HORSE OF THE HOUSEHOLD CAVALRY
Today the drum horse is only used during processions, but before the time of the armored tank and the airplane, the beating of drums and the blowing of trumpets were always used to give men courage as they were led into battle. These drums were presented by King William IV in England to the Life Guards regiment of his Household Cavalry in 1830.

Fifteen-year-old blue roan Clydesdale carrying rider and two pure silver drums, from the Household Cavalry of Queen Elizabeth II of Great Britain and the Commonwealth

The first ambulances, like this one from World War I, were harnessed to a pair of horses or mules

Red Cross flag

Whiffletree to which horse's harness was hitched to vehicle

Brake

Small front wheel to allow sharp turning

Large rear wheel to carry heavy loads

INTO BATTLE
The Charge of the Light Brigade – which resulted in huge casualties of both horses and men – was the most disastrous battle of the Crimean War (1853–1856), fought between Russia on one side and Britain, Turkey, France, and Sardinia on the other. The Crimea is a small area of land to the north of the Black Sea in the Ukraine.

TIBETAN WARRIOR
For hundreds of years, the Tibetan cavalry used a form of armor made of small metal plates (lamellae) laced together with leather thongs. This type of armor, for both horse and rider, had been used by the nomadic warriors of central Asia and was very similar to that worn by the Mongols when they overran Asia and Eastern Europe (pp. 32–33). The Tibetans have preserved this traditional armor – even into the 20th century.

Metal chanfron for protecting horse's head

Crinet for protecting horse's neck

Peytral to protect horse's chest

Leather lace

Small metal plate

Crupper protecting horse's hind quarters

Tibetan cavalry armor, for horse and rider, used between the 17th and 19th centuries

AUSTRALIAN ARTILLERY
The Waler (named after New South Wales in Australia, where horses were first imported 200 years ago) was the world's finest cavalry horse during World War I. These horses were strong and hardy and had good stamina and an amiable temperament. Now the Australian Stock Horse, based on the Waler, is used widely on cattle stations (ranches) for herding.

Nineteenth-century British cavalry spur, made of nickel silver

STURDY STIRRUPS
The stirrup was the most important innovation in the history of the horse in war, because it enabled a heavily armed rider to stay on his horse. Shown here is an 18th-century British cavalry stirrup made of brass.

NECESSITIES OF WAR
No battle could be fought without supplies of food, water, and arms hauled to the front line by pack-horses and mules.

Whiffletree

Tongue

Metal barrel containing water for either troops or animals

World War I water wagon hauled by two horses, made in England and used in France

GHANIAN WARRIOR
This brass model of a warrior on horseback was cast in Ghana in West Africa during the 18th century.

The age of chivalry

THE POLITICS OF EUROPE was dominated by the feudal system during the 11th and 12th centuries. Some knights were feudal lords, who owned tracts of land and granted its use to their vassals (servants). They also owned serfs (slaves) over whom they had complete power. These knights were Christians, bound by the code of chivalry – a religious, moral, and social code that covered every aspect of their lives. The ideal knight was brave, courteous, and honorable and totally dedicated to war against all non-Christians. By 1200, much of Europe was settled under feudalism, and armed knights began the conquest of new lands in the east. The Crusades were fought over territory – the Christians were trying to take the Holy Land back from the Muslims – but religious passion and the principles of chivalry meant that leaders, such as Richard the Lion-Hearted, could depend on their knights to give up their lives for the cause.

SAMURAI WARRIOR
This screen painting depicts a 12th-century Japanese samurai warrior going into battle. The honorable samurai, who wore two swords and a distinctive headdress, was totally loyal to his feudal lord.

European late 19th-century brass copy of 15th-century medieval spur with rowel (pp. 30–31), which had to be long to reach under the horse's armor

Blunted wood lance

Lambrequin, or mantling

Leather gauntlet, or glove

Cloth surcoat

Caparison, a colorfully decorated horse covering

Chain-mail armor

THE ROMANCE OF THE JOUST
Armed knights learned how to fight on horseback in tournaments. This sport, known as "justing," or "jousting" (from the Latin *juxtare*, meaning to clash), was part of the code of chivalry. The heavily armed knights tried to win points by either unhorsing their opponents or by breaking their own lances (up to 8 ft/2.5 m long) against the other's shields. From the dangerous hand-to-hand fighting, or melees, of the 12th century to the colorful pageantry of the 15th and 16th centuries, competitive tournaments were very popular spectator sports until their decline during the 17th century.

An early 14th-century reconstruction of a pair of sporting jousters

ARMOR FIT FOR A KING
Henry VIII of England passed laws to increase the size of horses by preventing the breeding of small stock. At the time of his reign in the early 1500s, the cannon had taken over as the principal weapon of war, against which heavy armor was no defense, but this armor was still used in royal parades.

Bronze eye guard for protecting a horse's face, England, 1st century A.D.

This full horse armor (or bard), known as the "Burgundian Bard," was given by Emperor Maximilian I of the Holy Roman Empire to Henry VIII. It was embossed, engraved, and silvered by Henry's Flemish harness gilder, c. 1515.

FULL METAL CHANFRON
This 16th-century Turkish chanfron (head armor for a horse) was made of gilt-copper, or tombac. It was part of a monument to the Ottoman Empire (late 1200s to early 1900s) that was set up in Agia Irene, a Byzantine church in Istanbul, Turkey.

Wood or leather crest in the shape of a bird or other animal was sometimes worn here

Metal helm

LEG GUARD
Wooden German jousting saddle (c. 1500) used with blunted lances in a "joust of peace" (war games). The two bows curved around the knight's thighs and protected him since he wore no leg armor, but he could not be unseated from his mount. Opponents' horses wore "blind" chanfrons; otherwise they would scare.

Vamplate, or metal disk, for protecting hand

Curb bit

Shield painted in heraldic colors, repeated on horse's caparison

COEUR DE LION
Richard the Lion-Hearted (1157–1199) became king of England in 1189. In 1190, he embarked on the Third Crusade to Palestine, where his bravery gave him immortal fame. He returned to England and spent the rest of his life warring against France.

STOP THAT HORSE
Four-spiked, iron caltrops (English, 1st–2nd century A.D.) were placed in the ground to lame the enemy's horses when they stepped on them.

Traveling by horse

Horses, asses, and mules have been used to transport people and their goods from place to place for more than 4,000 years. The first harness and carts had to be made entirely of wood, bone, and leather, until about 3,500 years ago, when people developed the use of copper and bronze, followed by iron about 2,000 years ago. The use of metals for parts of the harness, like rein rings (terrets) and bits, and on carts for the rims of wheels and for hubs and axles, greatly increased the efficiency and speed of transportation, especially in southern Europe and Asia, where the climate is dry. But in northern Europe, with its high rainfall, the packhorse remained the most practical means of travel (especially in winter) until roads were built, first by the Romans, and then not again until late in the Middle Ages (A.D. 1100–1500).

FIT FOR A QUEEN
This is a replica of Queen Elizabeth I's carriage – the first carriage to be built for the British monarchy. Before this time, royalty had to ride in carts. Made of wood, with steps that folded up to form part of the side, the carriage's padded roof provided protection from the rain.

HIGHWAYMAN AND HORSE
Dick Turpin (1706–1739) was an English highwayman who, according to legend, rode to the city of York in record time on his mount Black Bess.

BAREBACK RIDER
An 11th-century legend records that Lady Godiva rode naked through Coventry in a protest against heavy taxes imposed by her husband.

HORSE FEATHERS
The horses of the Native Americans had endless endurance and great stamina for use in both war and hunting. Color and decoration were part of the Native American's culture. The chiefs would wear magnificent feathered headdresses, and they would adorn their horses as well.

Blinker

Blaze

Bit with a straight bar

Collar

Metal hame with twist at top as traditional Gypsy decoration

Leather trace

BEAST OF BURDEN
This stone frieze shows that about 2,600 years ago, the ancient Assyrians bred powerful mules (pp. 26–27) to carry their hunting gear.

TRAVELING GYPSY
For hundreds of years, Gypsies have traveled around Europe, living in their caravans. No one knows where they came from, though they may be from northern India originally. Today, in some countries, people use these horse-drawn vehicles for vacations.

PATRON SAINT
St. Christopher (3rd century A.D.) was the patron saint of travelers – his feast day is July 25. A St. Christopher's medal has always been a symbol of good luck.

18th-century bronze horse and rider from Nigeria in West Africa

PILGRIMS' PROGRESS
Pilgrims to Thomas à Becket's shrine, at Canterbury Cathedral in England, were immortalized by the English poet Geoffrey Chaucer (c. 1345–1400), in his legendary *Canterbury Tales*.

Canvas-covered barrel top

Shaft

Sock

Nine-year-old Irish Draft horse (wearing traditional Gypsy harness) pulling a Gypsy caravan, built in Ireland, c. 1850

Horse-drawn vehicles

Snow sled with fur-lined seats for passengers and driver, built in the Netherlands, c. 1880

Bronze model of horse and carriage, Eastern Han dynasty of China, 2nd century A.D.

THE EARLIEST CHARIOTS in the ancient world had solid wood wheels that turned around a fixed axle. The invention of light, spoked wheels, like those shown here, meant that the chariot or carriage could travel much faster. The four-wheeled carriage with a swiveling axle that could turn independently of the body was a further improvement that became common only c. A.D. 500–1000. Just as today people show their status in society by the kind of automobile they own, in the past they did the same with their horse and carriage. The poor traveled in carts and on horse buses, and the rich traveled in fancy carriages harnessed to the most perfect horses. Great effort went into maintaining horses, harness, and carriages. Horses had to be fed and fitted with shoes by blacksmiths (which is the origin of the common English surname Smith), wheels had to be greased and repaired (giving another popular surname, Wheeler), and the carriages had to be kept clean and dry.

Elegant and expensive carriage harnessed to a pair of beautifully turned out horses

WHOSE LAND IS IT ANYWAY?
The early European immigrants who traveled across North America by stagecoach were often attacked by Native Americans on horseback, armed with stolen or bartered guns, as depicted in this painting by artist George Inness (1854–1926).

Blinker

Crupper

Check or driving rein

Hame

Collar

Terret

Bit

Martingale

Girth strap

Hip strap

Trace

Tongue

Triple whiffletree connecting two pairs of horses to stagecoach

Only one seat left on this overcrowded horse bus – two people will be disappointed

Driver's seat

Seating for two passengers

A type of Victorian carriage called a barouche, made in England based on a French design, c. 1880

WAY OUT WEST

Two businessmen – Henry Wells (1805–1878) and William Fargo (1818–1881) – opened their offices in San Francisco in 1852 to provide banking and shipping services, linking the Far West with the rest of the nation. The famous Wells, Fargo stagecoaches would carry private passengers, mail, money, and other valuables.

Jehu, or driver

Guard-messenger riding shotgun

Extra luggage stowed on top

Roll-up leather curtains to let in cool air or to keep out snow and rain

Brake lever operated by driver's foot

Seating inside for nine passengers – three each on three benches

Two sets of reins connecting the two pairs to driver

WELLS FARGO & CO. OVERLAND STAGE

U.S. MAIL

Passengers' luggage stowed in rear trunk

Step for passengers getting into stagecoach

Box under driver's seat containing tools, water bucket, mail pouches, and strongboxes full of valuables

Standing room for up to 12 passengers

Driver's seat

Two pairs of Welsh Cobs hauling Wells, Fargo stagecoach, made in U.S., late 1800s

Hunting brake, with driver's seat and space for standing room only, made in England, c. 1880

Heavy horses

In Europe and Asia, "the age of the horse" lasted from the classical times of Greece and Rome until the beginning of the 19th century. During this long period, until they were overtaken by the steam locomotive, not only were the horse, mule, and donkey the primary means of transportation, they were also necessary for all kinds of agricultural work. They were used for forestry, harvesting, pulling brewers' drays (low carts), and threshing grain, as well as for drawing water from wells. In the Mediterranean and Middle East areas, where the soils are light and dry, the donkey (pp. 24–25) carried out these tasks. In northern Europe, where the soils are damp and full of sticky clay, powerful heavy horses were needed for plowing and hauling heavy loads along muddy roads. Today, the heavy horses of Britain and Europe are exported around the world – to Canada, the U.S., Australia, and Japan.

HAYMAKING IN IRELAND
The horse and the donkey are still used on small farms in Ireland. Here in Connemara, County Galway, a wagon is being loaded with stooks of hay which will provide food for the farm animals during the winter.

Long, arched neck with thick mane

Fine head with straight profile

BELGIAN COMPACT
Also called a Brabant, this ancient breed of magnificent heavy draft horses from Belgium has remained purebred. They are still used as farm horses and are particularly popular in the U.S.

Decorated mane

Decorative brass

Hame, on heavy collar

Broad, deep-chested body

Chestnut-colored
Belgian Draft horse

BEFORE THE TRACTOR
The invention of the rigid, padded horse collar by the Chinese, c. A.D. 500, spread across Asia to Europe. The subsequent effect on agriculture was enormous, and horse-drawn plows became the tractors of their day. Nowadays, plowing with horses is slower than using a tractor, but some farmers find it more satisfying work; it is also better for the land. Plowing competitions still take place each year at agricultural shows in Britain, Europe, and North America, as shown here with these two superb Shire horses (left).

Strong, muscular leg

No feathering on heel of foot

Dapple-gray Percheron

Bridle

Collar

Saddle

Hip strap

Breech band

WHITBREAD

Loin strap

Chain trace

MOUNTAIN CLIMBER
The Avelignese is raised in the mountains of Italy. Used as both a draft horse and a packhorse, it is a bigger version of the Haflinger from Austria (pp. 38–39) and measures up to 14.3 hands (59 in/150 cm).

Chestnut-colored Avelignese

A BETTER BREW
Around 1800, the horse became increasingly important in the brewing industry – even the smallest company would have horses, drays, and carts, as well as a blacksmith and wheelwright. Horses were also used for grinding the malt and for driving water pumps. On beer deliveries, the horses' harness was heavily decorated.

Gray-colored Boulonnais

Chestnut-colored Suffolk Punch

FRENCH PRIDE
The head of the Boulonnais – a native of northwest France like the Percheron – shows the influence of its Arabian ancestry. This well-muscled, silky-coated ancient breed usually stands over 16 hands (64 in/163 cm).

A POWERFUL PUNCH
This breed – the Suffolk Punch – was developed as a farm horse in the county of Suffolk in eastern England during the late 1700s. Not only does it have fantastic stamina and power, but it also needs less food than other heavy breeds. The Suffolk's coloring is always chestnut, but the shade can vary from light to dark.

Long, powerful hindquarters

BEST OF FRANCE
The Percheron, from northern France, is perhaps the best known of all breeds of heavy horse. Its elegance, despite its great size, is due to crossbreeding with Arabian stallions. It is a very popular breed around the world, particularly in the U.S. and Canada.

AFTER THE HARVEST IS DONE
Every fall for centuries, horses have been used to prepare the ground for the next season's crops after the harvest. Here this 16th-century Flemish scene shows horses used for plowing and harrowing (smoothing the plowed earth).

DEEP IN THE FOREST
Heavy horses have traditionally been used for hauling heavy logs out of the forest, as shown by these Shire horses in southern England.

Horse-drawn rake for gathering cut hay into long, smooth rows

Horse power

WITHOUT THE HORSE, the industrial revolution at the end of the 18th century could never have taken place. Transportation by horse enabled manufactured goods to be carried to ships for export to foreign countries, and it enabled people to flock to the cities for work in the new industries. Horses were used in the factories to provide power to engines and machines for grinding malt for brewing (pp. 50–51) or wheat for flour, for spinning cotton, and for furnace blowing. In the mines, ponies were used underground for hauling loads from the coal seams (pp. 62–63), and aboveground for towing barges full of coal along the canals. Horses also hauled buses, fire engines, and supply wagons. Today, there are few places where the horse has not been replaced by machinery, but the term used to measure the pulling power of an engine is still "horsepower." One horsepower is equivalent to 746 watts, and one metric horsepower equals 736 watts.

Cog

HORSE BUSES
The first public horse carriages in Britain started in 1564, but the roads were so bad that people could not travel far, especially in winter.

Weighing scales

COAL MERCHANT
THOMAS JEWELL

Heavily laden coal wagon, made in England, 1920

Shaft attached to grinding stones

Sack of coal

Brake

SNOWSHOES
In heavy snow, a sturdy team of surefooted horses is needed to haul logs out of forests or sleds full of people or goods, as shown by these Haflinger ponies in Bavaria in southern Germany.

Lamp

Horn

Water hose

EXPLORING THE INTERIOR
Teams of horses hauled wood wagons laden with supplies to Australia's interior, such as this area of New South Wales. The safety of these wagons depended on the wheels being made correctly.

Water bucket

LONDON

Victorian fire engine, English, 1890 – wheels were wide to allow horses to turn corners sharply without risking a spill

Giant iron flywheel attached to an iron shaft, or rod

GOING AROUND IN CIRCLES
The tediousness of this circular work is all the more apparent when viewed from above.

Heavy collar

Whiffletree attached to iron bar, in turn linked to shaft

Metal linked-chain trace

Long, well-muscled leg helping horse pull heavy load

Huge, flat grinding stones hidden underground

Shire horse pulling heavy horse gin, or horse wheel, inside a circular building called a roundhouse

TOWING A BARGE
Horses and mules (pp. 26–27) were often used to pull barges heavily laden with coal or farm produce down rivers and canals in Europe – an efficient means of transportation that lasted well into the 20th century.

A HARD GRIND
This horse is being used to turn a mill wheel to grind corn into flour – just as horses, mules (pp. 26–27), and donkeys (pp. 24–25) have done all over Europe since Roman times. The animals were forced to walk around and around in a small circle for hours on end, pulling the rope or chain that turned the heavy grinding stone. Sometimes, a pair of horses would carry out this operation – they had to be specially trained to keep to a steady pace and at the correct speed.

Light draft work

THEY MAY NOT BE AS ELEGANT as the Thoroughbred or as magnificent as the heavy horse (pp. 50–53), but the common light draft horses were the mainstay of transportation throughout the world until the development of the steam locomotive in the 1820s. Light draft horses pulled every kind of wagon, cart, and carriage. These horses had to be powerful and fast, as well as able to cover long distances without becoming tired. Most of them did not belong to any particular breed, but some – like the Cleveland Bay of Yorkshire in northern England – had been preserved as pure breeds since ancient times. Originally, Cleveland Bays were known as "Chapman horses" because they were used to carry the loads of traveling salesmen, or "chapmen," around the countryside.

Hansom cab (c. 1850), designed for two passengers, driven by single driver and horse

CROWD CONTROL
The specially trained horses of mounted police still perform an important function in being able to move fast through crowds of people. They provide their riders with mobility and a good view of events.

Feathered plume

PACKHORSE
For centuries, horses have been used for carrying heavy loads on their backs. This woodcutter's horse in Guatemala is laden with planks of wood.

Pole strap attaching collar to central shaft (pole)

Royal coat of arms

Barred Victorian wagon used to carry prisoners, made in England, c. 1890

Black velvet pall, or blanket, covering horse's hindquarters

DAYS OF MOURNING
In the old days, a black-draped hearse, drawn by a pair of black-plumed horses, was an impressive sight as it slowly carried the coffin to a funeral.

SUNDAY MORNING DRIVE
A family enjoys an outing in their horse-drawn carriage in this print by lithographers Nathaniel Currier (1813–1888) and James Ives (1824–1895).

Harness attached to center pole

Pair of grays and phaeton, English, c. 1840

REGENCY RAKE ABOUT TOWN
In English spa towns in the early part of the 19th century, young gentlemen would dash about town driving their latest status symbol, such as this convertible model – an elegant sporting phaeton driven with the top up or down.

Plumes made of ostrich feathers

Driver dressed in dark mourning suit

Coffin

Engraved glass sides

Splinter bar to which traces are attached

Pair of black Welsh Cobs, in black and silver harness, pulling funeral hearse, made in England, c. 1850

R. JORDAN & SONS
THE PADDOCK

Rubber-wheeled dairy wagon, made in England, c. 1950

The horse in North America

THE INDIGENOUS (NATIVE) WILD HORSES of North America became extinct about 10,000 years ago. The first domestic horses landed on the continent with Christopher Columbus in 1492. Since then horses have symbolized freedom and enterprise in North America, and for the next 425 years the rise in the horse population matched that of the human population. Horses have been used by nearly everyone – they have drawn heavy loads in the searing heat of deserts, down deep mines, and along muddy roads. The horse transformed the lives of Native Americans, who had previously hauled their possessions by dogsled and on their own backs. With the horse, the native peoples had a new means of fast transportation and could also hunt buffalo more efficiently.

BUFFALO BILL
In 1882, former Pony Express rider (pp. 62–63) Buffalo Bill Cody (1846–1917) put on the first professional rodeo show at the Fourth of July celebrations in Nebraska, with contests in shooting, riding, and broncobusting.

TRAVEL TODAY
The Amish settled in Pennsylvania in the early 1700s and developed the Conestoga (a heavier version of the covered wagon), which helped explore the West (pp. 34–35). Today their simple lifestyle means that they still use horses for both work and travel.

A MUSICAL RIDE
The Royal Canadian Mounted Police (founded in 1873) are world famous for their splendid pageantry – red tunics, black horses, and bright banners.

Stetson hat

Fringed leather jacket

Striped saddle-cloth

High pommel of Western saddle

Riding whip

Black-and-white-striped mane

Curb bit

LEGENDARY LADIES
Calamity Jane, Annie Oakley, Belle Starr . . . the list of female legends of the Old West is endless when cowgirls had to ride a horse, shoot a gun, and cope with everything as well as any man. The bad guys and girls – like Frank and Jesse James, the Dalton gang, Billy the Kid, and Flo Quick – were chased by lawmen like Wyatt Earp and Wild Bill Hickok, and everyone rode a horse.

Leather chaps

Leather stirrups

The Appaloosa, with its distinctive spotted coat (pp. 40–41), was a favorite mount of Native Americans.

Cowgirl in typical Western clothes riding 14-year-old skewbald pony

STAMPEDE!
Every July at the Calgary Stampede in Canada, the contests of skill and speed at this rodeo include the dramatic chuck (food) wagon races. Two pairs of horses, a cook–driver, and four outriders race around a circuit – the first across the finish line wins.

Lasso for roping cattle

Stetson

Pommel

Silver and tooled-leather gun belt

HOLLYWOOD HEROES
"There isn't a bronc that can't be rode; there isn't a cowboy that can't be throwed." The central feature of the rodeo show is the bucking horse, symbol of humans' need to conquer the wild and the free, but a horse is not "broken" without a fight. Wild-horse races are also a feature of some rodeos, in which unbroken horses are saddled and ridden to show off the cowboys' courage. Movie cowboys and their famous horses – such as the Lone Ranger and Silver, Roy Rogers and Trigger – helped to recreate the legend of the Old West.

Curb bit

BUFFALO HUNT
In this painting by artist George Catlin (1796–1872), the Native Americans' horses are shown hunting the buffalo – which all but disappeared from the West through excessive slaughter by European immigrants.

PAUL REVERE'S RIDE
Famous for his ride from Boston on the night of April 18, 1775, to warn the colonists of Massachusetts that the British troops were coming, Paul Revere (1735–1818) and his borrowed horse have become an American legend.

Leather chaps

Leather stirrups

ARMY ROUGHRIDERS
Ordinary cavalrymen (an army's mounted forces) had to spend long hours in the saddle, so it was important to have strong horses. In this painting by artist Frederic Remington (1861–1909), the U.S. Cavalry is in hot pursuit.

Cowboy on palomino (part Thoroughbred, part Arabian)

Sporting horses

"THEY RAPIDLY FLEW OVER THE PLAIN, swiftly . . . while their manes were tossed about by the breath of the wind." This description of a chariot race comes from Homer's *Iliad* (written in the 8th century B.C.), in which five Greek warriors raced across the plain of Troy in honor of the hero Patroclus, killed in the Trojan War. In the 7th century B.C. four-horse chariot races were part of the early Olympic Games, and during the next several centuries the Romans raced horses in a "circus," or special arena. From the end of the Roman Empire, horse-riding competitions became less popular until the Middle Ages. Then, in the late 11th century, the first flat racing began in England; later, in Renaissance Europe, riding schools teaching classical equitation developed. In 1750 the first Jockey Club was founded in England, and by 1775 trotting races began in Russia. Today, equestrian sports are as popular as ever, and much money is invested in breeding racehorses.

Every year in Siena, Italy, horses and riders race around the main square in the dramatic and exciting *Palio*

Circus Horse, by French painter Georges Seurat (1859–1891)

Pommel

Cantle

Metal stirrup

A smooth leather English saddle has a very low cantle and pommel

There is a legend that Pelops, here driving a four-horse chariot, founded the Olympic Games in 1222 B.C. to honor the supreme deity, Zeus

Special hard hat

Formal riding jacket

Throatlatch

Curb rein

Browband

Cheekpiece

Noseband

Numnah

Painted wood barrier at least 4.5 ft (1.4 m) high

Seven-year-old dapple gray jumper – a mix of Irish Draft and Irish Thoroughbred

POINT TO POINT
Steeplechasing began in 1752 as a cross-country race in which a church steeple was the goal and all the hedges, or gates, in between had to be jumped to reach it.

OVER THEY GO
To jump over obstacles in their path is part of the natural behavior of wild horses that are galloping away from a predator. But domesticated horses will only jump when directed to do so by their riders. To train a horse to be a show jumper is a long and complicated process.

IN COLD WATER
Three-day eventing tests the endurance, speed, and obedience of a horse, as well as its rider's ability. The event is broken down into dressage on the first day, followed by a cross-country and steeplechase course that includes a spectacular water hazard (as shown), with show jumping on the third and final day.

FUN FOR EVERYONE
Gymkhanas, or mounted games, offer young riders a chance to see what they and their ponies can do at this junior level of equestrian, or horse-riding, competition.

Riding side saddle originated with European royalty some 600 years ago, but in 19th-century England ladies rode this way for the hunt

Saddle horn

High cantle

Lariat

Classic jodphurs, or riding pants

English saddle

Leather stirrup

Western saddles, made of heavy tooled leather, have distinctive pommels (saddle horns) on which cowboys' lariats (lassos) hang

Bridoon rein

Bridoon

Overreach bands to protect front feet from hind feet

Girth

Metal stirrup

ANYONE FOR POLO?
Polo, as seen in this 17th-century silk print, was invented by the Chinese about 2,500 years ago. Today it is very popular in Argentina, the U.S., Australia, and Britain. Two teams of four players each hit the ball with long-handled mallets and try to score as many goals as possible in seven and a half minutes (a "chukker"). There can be from four to six chukkers in a match. The team with the most goals wins the match.

THEY'RE OFF!
Modern flat racing – racing on a track with no obstacles – owes its existence to the Thoroughbred (pp. 38–39), first developed in Britain during the 17th and 18th centuries. Today influential racing nations include Britain, France, Italy, Australia, and the U.S.

Horses for courses

THE CLOSE BOND that has been forged over thousands of years between humans and their horses cannot be broken by the growth of the automobile industry. Today the horse is becoming ever more popular in competitive sports, and those who cannot take part in show jumping or racing get much pleasure from watching them on television. Most highly bred horses, in particular racehorses and jumpers, spend exhausting hours each day in extensive training. When they are taken out for an event they will use their natural instincts to follow a leader (the other horses), helped by the sting of a whip (which has the same effect as a pursuing predator). Besides racing or jumping, the most ancient sport involving horses is hunting. Many people consider this is cruel to the prey, but others feel that hunting protects the landscape by controlling the numbers of fox and deer. In addition to hunting, horses (singly or in teams) provide an amazing variety of sport and recreation for thousands of people around the world – from pony trekking and endurance racing to international driving and classical equitation, or dressage.

AWAY TO THE RACES
Flat racing – the "sport of kings" – is very popular around the world in such classic races as England's Derby, America's Belmont Stakes, and Australia's Melbourne Cup. Here the French Impressionist painter Edgar Degas (1834–1917) shows jockeys and horses in their owners' racing colors awaiting their call to the start line.

Height at withers 15 hands (60 in/ 152 cm)

CROSSING A CREEK
All around the world, pony trekking is a popular recreation for both adults and children. In this picture children are riding their ponies in single file across a shallow stream in the Victorian Alps in southeastern Australia.

PACERS AND TROTTERS
In many parts of the world, including North America, France, Russia, Australia, and New Zealand, the trotting or harness race is just as popular as flat racing. The modern trotting race is similar to the ancient chariot race, except that it is run with a single horse that is only allowed to trot. In pacing (as shown here), the legs move in lateral (same side) rather than diagonal pairs (legs move in diagonal pairs for conventional trotting).

THREE HORSEMEN
For centuries, riders took part in long-distance races to see who could break the latest time and distance record. In this 18th-century Japanese print by Katsushika Hokusai (1760–1849), three horsemen are racing to the foothills of Mt. Fuji.

Three-year-old bay American Standardbred driven by owner in his racing colors

ELEGANT DRESSAGE
Classical riding shows the horse at its peak of fitness and obedience to its rider. Dressage reached its height of popularity in the 18th century. In modern advanced dressage competitions, marks out of ten are given for excellence. One of the most difficult movements (shown here) is changing the leading leg with every stride at the canter.

HAVE YOU PASSED YOUR DRIVING TEST YET?
At horse shows around the world, driving events are very popular. In 1970 the first international horse driving trials, based on the format of the three-day event, took place. These trials had presentation and dressage on the first day, followed by a marathon of 17 miles (27 km), and then obstacle driving on the final day.

For centuries, horsehair from the horse's tail has been used for stringing bows of musical instruments, such as the cello

THE HUNTERS RETURN
People have hunted from horseback since the time of the Assyrians, c. 2500 B.C., when the prey was lions or wild oxen. Later, in Europe, as shown in this 16th-century Flemish calendar, the quarry was a stag, bear, or hare. In the 17th century the English developed fox hunting with the help of specially trained scent hounds, and it is still a popular sport there as well as in the eastern U.S.

Riding whip

Jockey cap

Shirt showing owner's racing colors

Sulky, or cart

Special harness around legs to help horse maintain its lateral pacing

Walking the horse
The horse has four natural gaits – the walk, trot, canter, and gallop. The walk has four beats – left hind, left fore, right hind, and right fore legs, each hitting the ground separately. The trot has two beats – left hind and right fore together, then right hind and left fore together. The canter has three beats – left hind, then left fore and right hind together, and finally the right fore leg. The gallop has four beats – the same as the walk – then all four feet come off the ground.

Useful ponies

Children who learn to ride and care for a pony develop an understanding of the rich relationships that can exist between humans and animals, and a pony can often be a child's best friend. In the past, the native ponies of northern Europe were used as pack animals and for general farm work, and then when a particularly docile pony was too old to work, it was given to a small child for the first riding lessons. In those times almost everyone knew how to handle a horse. Today, fewer people learn to ride and even fewer have a pony of their own, but for those who do, it is a most rewarding experience. Most breeds, like the Dartmoor and Fell ponies, are extremely hardy and have evolved in a harsh environment where they survive on little food and remain outdoors all winter. However, thoroughbred ponies that are trained for the show ring need much more care.

THROUGH ALL KINDS OF WEATHER
From Missouri to California, Pony Express riders braved bad weather, difficult terrain, and attacks from Native Americans to carry the mail 2,000 miles (3,300 km) across the U.S. in the 1860s. They managed to cut delivery time from weeks to just days.

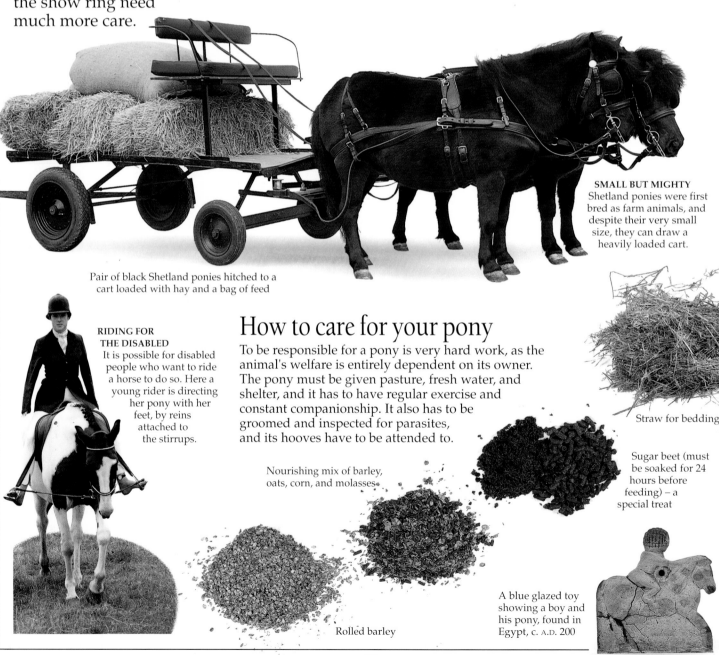

SMALL BUT MIGHTY
Shetland ponies were first bred as farm animals, and despite their very small size, they can draw a heavily loaded cart.

Pair of black Shetland ponies hitched to a cart loaded with hay and a bag of feed

RIDING FOR THE DISABLED
It is possible for disabled people who want to ride a horse to do so. Here a young rider is directing her pony with her feet, by reins attached to the stirrups.

How to care for your pony

To be responsible for a pony is very hard work, as the animal's welfare is entirely dependent on its owner. The pony must be given pasture, fresh water, and shelter, and it has to have regular exercise and constant companionship. It also has to be groomed and inspected for parasites, and its hooves have to be attended to.

Straw for bedding

Sugar beet (must be soaked for 24 hours before feeding) – a special treat

Nourishing mix of barley, oats, corn, and molasses

Rolled barley

A blue glazed toy showing a boy and his pony, found in Egypt, c. A.D. 200

Various types of rugs or sheets (made from jute, wool, or nylon) may be needed for keeping the horse warm in winter or protecting it from flies and dust in hot weather

Halter for training horse to stand tied

Dressage whip

Lunge whip

AROUND AND AROUND
Most fairgrounds have a merry-go-round, or carousel, where children can safely ride a brightly painted mechanical horse that goes up and down as well as around and around.

Shedding brush

Hoof oil

Curry comb for mane, tail, and body

Soft body brush

Metal comb for tail and mane

Hay for eating

Miner's lamp

PIT PONIES
Ponies that were blind were often taken to work down in mines, as they did not need to see their way along the tunnels. It was wet, cold, and dark in the coal mines of the old days, and it was the hardest of all lives for both the miners and their ponies, many of which lived underground for months on end.

A young boy and his dark gray Shetland pony ready for working underground in a coal mine

Three-tined fork for mucking (cleaning) out stables

Index

A

Alexander the Great 33, 42
American Standardbred 60
Amish 56
Anchitherium 9
Andalusian horse 34, 40–41
Appaloosa horse 56
Arabian 38–39, 42, 51, 57
armor, horse 42–45
asses 6–8, 12, 14, 16–17, 24,
    30, 42, 46; African 7, 16,
    22, 24; Asian 7, 16
Australian Stock Horse
    (Waler) 43
Avelignese horse 51

B

Barb 38–39, 41
Basuto ponies 40
Battle of Hastings 31
bay color 38–40
behavior 12–13, 40
Belgian Draft horse
    (Brabant) 50
birth 14–15
bits 25–26, 30–31, 38–40,
    45–46, 48, 54, 56–57;
    curb 31, 45, 56–57;
    pelham 31; snaffle 31
Black Bess 46
black coat 41, 55
Black Hawk, Chief 34
blacksmith 28–29
bones 8–11, 21
Boulonnais horse 51
brands 23
bridle 25–26, 30–31, 33,
    38–39, 42, 51, 53
brown coat 38, 40
brumbies 36
Bucephalus 33
Buffalo Bill Cody 56

C

Camargue horses 37
carriages 22, 27, 46, 48–49,
    52, 54–55
carts 24, 26, 46–47, 54–55

Catlin, George 57
cavalry 42–43, 57
centaur 22
Cervantes, Miguel 42
chariots 22, 26, 33, 42, 48, 58
Charlemagne 32
Chaucer, Geoffrey 47
chestnut color 38–41,
    50–51
chestnut tree 11
chuck wagon race 57
circus horses 39, 58
Cleveland Bay 38, 54
Clydesdale 42
Cob 49, 55–56; Welsh 49, 55
collar, invention of 50
Columbus, Christopher 56
conformation 40
Connemara pony 38
Cortés, Hernando 34
covered wagon 35
cowboys 35, 56–57
Currier & Ives 55

D

Danish Warmblood 40
dapple-gray color 38–39,
    50, 58
Dartmoor pony 62
Degas, Edgar 60
donkey 7, 12, 16–17,
    21–22, 24–27, 30, 42, 50,
    53; Irish 25; Poitou 7, 25
Don Quixote 42
draft horses 38, 50–55
dressage 31, 59–61
drum horse 42
Dülmen ponies 36
dun color 41

E

Elizabeth I 46
Elizabeth II 42
endurance racing 59–60
Eohippus 8
Equidae 6, 8, 10, 12
Equus 6, 8–9, 20–21, 24
evolution 8–9
Exmoor pony 20

F

face markings 6, 34, 37, 40,
    46, 57

Falabella 40–41
farming 6–7, 50–51
Fell ponies 36, 62
feral horses 14, 20, 36–37, 57
flat racing 58–60
foal 7, 10–11, 14–15, 24
fossils 8–9, 20
French Trotter 38
Friesian horse 41

G

gaits 61
gauchos 35
Gelderland 35, 40
gelding 12
Genghis Khan 32
gestation 14, 24
ghorkhar 17
girth 6, 25–26, 34, 39, 48, 53
Godiva, Lady 46
gray color 38–40, 51, 55
gymkhanas 59
gypsy caravan 46–47

H

Haflinger ponies 38, 51–52
hands (height) 7
harness 17, 22, 24, 26,
    30–31, 34, 46–49, 50–55,
    60
heavy horses 50–53
Henry VIII 45
Herring, John 39
hinnies 26–27
Hipparion 8
Hippidion 8
hipposandal 29
Homer 22, 58
hooves 6–11, 18, 24–25,
    28–29, 38
horse sales 39
horsepower 52
horseshoe pitching 29
hunting 22–23, 46, 57, 60–61
Hyracotherium 8–9

I

Icelandic pony 12
Inness, George 48
international driving trials
    61
Irish Draft horse 47, 58
Irish Thoroughbred 58
Italian Heavy Draft horse
    41

J

jackass 27
Jacobson's organ 13
jennet 27
jenny donkey 24, 27
jousting 44–45

K

keratin 28
khur 17
kiang 16–17
Konik pony 20
kulan 7, 12, 17

L

leg markings 34, 38, 40, 47
light draft horses 54–55
Lipizzaner 31, 40
logging 51–52

M

Marc, Franz 41
Marengo 42
mares 12–14, 26
merry-go-round 63
Merychippus 8
Mesohippus 8–9
Morgan horse 40
mules 12, 18, 25–27, 34, 43,
    46, 50, 53
mustangs 36–37
muzzle 6–7, 15, 18, 20, 25,
    40
mythical horses 7, 22–23

N

Napoleon 42
New Forest ponies 37
Nonius horse 38
North American Indians
    30, 34, 46, 48, 56–57

O

Oldenburg 40
onager 7, 12, 16–17
Onohippidium 8
Oregon Trail 35
Orlov Trotter 38

P

pack animals 25–26, 46, 54
Palio race 58
Palomino color 14, 38, 57
Parahippus 8
Pegasus 22
Percheron 50–51
Perissodactyla 6
piebald 36, 41
Pinto pony 37, 41
pit ponies 52, 63
Pliohippus 8
plowing 50–51
points of the horse 6
police horses 54, 56
Polo, Marco 32
polo ponies 59
Pony Express 62
pony-trekking 60
Przewalski's horse 13,
    20–21, 36

Q

quagga 18–19

R

racehorse 10–11, 38, 58–60
rein ring 17, 31
reins 24–26, 30–31, 33–34,
    39, 42, 48–49, 58–59, 62
Remington, Frederic 57
Revere, Paul 57
Richard the Lion-Hearted
    44–45
roan color 41
rocking horse 6
rodeo 56–57
Rosinante 42

S

saddle 30–32, 42, 45, 51;
    English 58; Western
    56–57, 59
samurai 44
Scythian horsemen 30, 32,
    34
Shetland ponies 6, 41,
    62– 63
Shire horse 7, 15, 28–29,
    . 40, 50–51, 53
shoeing 28–29, 32, 35, 48
showjumping 58–60

sidesaddle 30–31, 59
skeleton 10–11, 21
skewbald 36, 39, 41, 56
skull 8–11
Spanish Riding School 40
sport 22, 32, 38, 44, 58–61
spotted coat 41
spurs 30, 42–44; prick 30;
    rowel 30
stagecoach 48–49
stallion 12–14, 26–27, 33, 38,
    40
steeplechase 58–59
St Christopher 47
St George 33
stirrups 30–32, 34, 40,
    42–43, 56–57, 59, 62
Stubbs, George 10–11
Suffolk Punch 51

T

tarpan 20
teeth 8–12, 18, 21
Thoroughbred 38, 54, 59, 62
three-day event 59
transportation 32, 46–56
trotting race 58, 60
Turpin, Dick 46

U

unicorn 7, 42

V

vehicles 34–35, 46–49, 54–55
Vikings 32

W

war 22–23, 27, 32, 42–45
Wells, Fargo 49
wild horses 20–21, 36–37
William IV 42
William the Conqueror 31

Z

zebras 6–8, 12, 14, 18–19;
    common 7, 14, 18–19;
    Grévy's 18–19; mountain
    18
zebroid 18
zedonk 19

Acknowledgments

Dorling Kindersley wish to thank:
Alan Hills, Dave Gowers, Christi
Graham, Sandra Marshall, Nick
Nicholls, and Barbara Winters of the
British Museum, and Colin Keates
of the Natural History Museum for
additional special photography.
Clubb Chipperfield Limited, Foxhill
Stables & Carriage Repository,
Suzanne Gill, Wanda Lee Jones of
the Welshpool Andalusian Stud,
Marwell Zoological Park, the
National Shire Horse Centre, Harry
Perkins, and the Whitbread Hop
Farm for lending animals and
vehicles for photography.
The Household Cavalry for
providing the rider and the drum
horse, and The Knights of Arkley
for the jousting sequence.
The Berrriewood Stud Farm,

Carol Johnson, and Plough Studios
for their help in providing arenas
and studios for photography.
Dr Alan Gentry of the Natural
History Museum, Christopher
Gravett of the Royal Armouries
(HM Tower of London), and
Rowena Loverance of the British
Museum for their research help.
Céline Carez, Hannah Conduct, Liz
Sephton, Christian Sévigny, Helena
Spiteri and Cheryl Telfer for
editorial and design assistance.
Jane Parker for the index.
Illustrations: John Woodcock

Picture credits
t=top, b=bottom, c=center, l=left, r=right
Aerofilms: 21tl
Allsport: 58tr Vandystadt; 59br Ben
Radford

American Museum of Natural History:
8cl, 9br
Ardea: 14clt, 14cl, 16c, 17cr Jean-Paul
Ferreo; 17bl Joanna van Grusen
Barnaby's Picture Library: 43cr, 45bl
Bridgeman Art Library: 41tl Archiv fur
Kunst & Geschichte, Berlin; 34bl
Biblioteca Nacional, Madrid; 24tr, 51cbr,
60c British Library; 49tl Guildhall
Library; 39cb Harrogate Museums and
Art Galleries; 35t, 41tl, 56tl, 59tc Private
Collection; 57ct Smithsonian Institution,
Washington, D.C.; 32bl Musée Condée,
Chantilly; 58tl (detail) Musée d'Orsay,
Paris; 60tr (detail) Louvre, Paris
Trustees of the British Museum: front
cover tl, 4ctr, 7br, 16tl, 17br, 22tl, 22cl,
22br, 23tr, 26c, 28c, 33tr, 33bl, 46bl
Bruce Coleman Ltd: 12bl C. Hughes; 18b
J. & D. Bartlett; 39tl C. Henneghien
Mike Dent: front cover cr, 23tl, 27tl, 46ctl,
50tr, 54cl, 63tr
Dorling Kindersley: 37tr Dave King (by
courtesy of the National Motor Museum,
Beaulieu); front cover, 27tr, 36tl, 38 (all
except 38br), 40bl, 41 (all except 41tl,
41br), 50c, 50–51b, 51tr, 51c, 51cr, 56bl,

63bc Bob Langrish
Mary Evans Picture Library: 23bl, 32tr
Robert Harding Picture Library: 21cr,
24cb, 48tr, 51bc, 56cr
Alan Hills: 20bl
Hirmer: 33tl
Michael Holford: 31tc, 44tl, 47tc, 59bl, 60tl
Hulton Picture Collection: 53b, 63bl
Frank Lane Picture Agency: 12br
Bob Langrish: 37tl, 40br, 41br, 54cr, 56cl,
57t, 58bc, 59tl, 59tr, 61tl, 61tc
The Mansell Collection: 42bl
Natural History Photographic Agency:
14br Patrick Fagot; 21br E. Hanumantha
Rao; 36bl, 60cl A.N.T.
Peter Newark's Western Americana: 34tr,
34cl, 43tl, 48cb, 55tl, 57cb, 57bl, 62t
Only Horses: 37c, 62bl
Oxford Scientific Films: 17tc/Anup Shah/
Okapia
Planet Earth: 19br Nick Greaves
Ann Ronan Picture Library: 6tr
The Board of Trustees of Royal
Armouries: 2c, 43cl, 45tc, 45cr
Whitbread Brewery: 13cr
Zefa: 12tr, 13tr, 24clt, 24bl, 25cr, 35br, 36cl,
46cb, 52cl, 52br